FLUENCY IN THE CLASSROOM

SOLVING PROBLEMS IN THE TEACHING OF LITERACY
Cathy Collins Block, Series Editor

Fluency
in the Classroom

Edited by

MELANIE R. KUHN
PAULA J. SCHWANENFLUGEL

THE GUILFORD PRESS
New York   London

© 2008 The Guilford Press
A Division of Guilford Publications, Inc.
72 Spring Street, New York, NY 10012
www.guilford.com

Printed in the United States of America

This book is printed on acid-free paper.

Last digit is print number: 9 8 7 6 5 4 3 2 1

Library of Congress Cataloging-in-Publication Data

Fluency in the classroom / edited by Melanie R. Kuhn, Paula J. Schwanenflugel.
     p. cm. — (Solving problems in the teaching of literacy)
  Includes bibliographical references and index.
  ISBN-13: 978-1-59385-573-4 (pbk. : alk. paper)
  ISBN-10: 1-59385-573-7 (pbk. : alk. paper)
  ISBN-13: 978-1-59385-574-1 (hardcover : alk. paper)
  ISBN-10: 1-59385-574-5 (hardcover : alk. paper)
  1. Oral reading. 2. Fluency (Language learning) 3. Reading (Primary) I. Kuhn,
Melanie R. II. Schwanenflugel, Paula J.
  LB1573.5.F58 2008
  372.4—dc22
                                                           2007028704

To the memory of Steven A. Stahl, who inspired us
to proceed on this fascinating topic of research

To our spouses, Jason Chambers and Will Whitman,
who supported us when we were excited, overwhelmed,
or forlorn about this work

To Emma Kuhn and James Costa,
who reminded Melanie that there is a world
beyond her laptop

And, finally, to Paula's children,
Paul and Steve Whitman, who became fluent
and accomplished readers while their mother
was carrying out research on fluency and editing
this book. They helped her keep it real.

We thank the children and teachers with whom
we have worked. They have informed our thinking
about reading fluency tremendously,
and made this book possible.

About the Editors

Melanie R. Kuhn, PhD, is Associate Professor at Rutgers—The State University of New Jersey. She began her teaching career in the Boston public schools, has worked as a literacy coordinator for an adult education program, and spent 3 years as a clinician at an international school in England. Dr. Kuhn received her EdM in Reading and Language at the Harvard Graduate School of Education, her MPhil in the Psychological Investigation of Intellectual Development at Cambridge University, and her PhD in Reading Education from the University of Georgia. She has authored several articles and chapters, including "Fluency: A Review of Developmental and Remedial Practices" with Steven A. Stahl, and currently teaches courses on assessing and correcting reading difficulties. Her research interests also include literacy instruction for struggling readers, comprehension development, and vocabulary instruction.

Paula J. Schwanenflugel, PhD, is Professor of Educational Psychology, Psychology, Linguistics, and Cognitive Science at the University of Georgia, where she teaches courses on child development, cognition, and psycholinguistics as applied to education. She has recently been engaged in grant research on reading fluency, preliteracy skills, vocabulary, and classroom practices related to these topics. Dr. Schwanenflugel served as principal investigator of an Interagency Educational Research Initiative grant to develop theory and classroom practices for reading fluency, funded through the National Institute of Child Health and Human Development and the National Science Foundation.

Contributors

Barbara A. Bradley, PhD, Department of Curriculum and Teaching, University of Kansas, Lawrence, Kansas

Eileen A. Cohen, MEd, Department of Psychology, Georgia State University, Atlanta, Georgia

Carolyn A. Groff, PhD, Department of Curriculum and Instruction, School of Education, Monmouth University, West Long Branch, New Jersey

Elfrieda H. Hiebert, PhD, Graduate School of Education, University of California, Berkeley, Berkeley, California

Melanie R. Kuhn, PhD, Department of Learning and Teaching, Graduate School of Education, Rutgers—The State University of New Jersey, New Brunswick, New Jersey

Maureen W. Lovett, PhD, Departments of Pediatrics and Psychology, University of Toronto, Toronto, Ontario, Canada

Elizabeth B. Meisinger, PhD, Department of Psychology, University of Memphis, Memphis, Tennessee

Justin Miller, PhD, Department of Educational Psychology, University of Georgia, Athens, Georgia

Robin D. Morris, PhD, Department of Psychology, Georgia State University, Atlanta, Georgia

Lesley Mandel Morrow, PhD, Department of Learning and Teaching, Graduate School of Education, Rutgers—The State University of New Jersey, New Brunswick, New Jersey

Matthew Quirk, PhD, Department of Counseling, Clinical, and School Psychology, Gevirtz Graduate School of Education, University of California, Santa Barbara, Santa Barbara, California

Hilary P. Ruston, PhD, Department of Educational Psychology, University of Georgia, Athens, Georgia

Paula J. Schwanenflugel, PhD, Department of Educational Psychology and Instructional Technology, University of Georgia, Athens, Georgia

Rose A. Sevcik, PhD, Department of Psychology, Georgia State University, Atlanta, Georgia

Katherine A. Dougherty Stahl, EdD, Steinhardt School of Education, New York University, New York, New York

Maryanne Wolf, PhD, Eliot–Pearson Department of Child Development, Tufts University, Medford, Massachusetts

Deborah G. Woo, EdD, Department of Literacy Education, New Jersey City University, Jersey City, New Jersey

Preface

One of the most important things you can do for your primary-grade students is help them become fluent readers. It is important for myriad reasons (e.g., National Reading Panel, 2000; Samuels, 2006). Fluent readers are able to recognize words not only accurately, but also quickly and effortlessly. They are also able to read passages with expression, making them sound like speech. And, because they do not need to expend a great deal of energy on either word recognition or determining appropriate phrasing, they are able to focus their attention on understanding what they are reading. (To better understand the nature of fluency and its role in the reading process, see Chapter 1.)

Recently, a number of books have dealt with reading fluency and ways to help learners become more fluent readers. So, why would we write another one? We wrote this book to describe two whole-class approaches to fluency development—approaches that can govern the shared reading component of your curriculum, allowing your students to all focus on the same text.[1] Unfortunately, many classrooms still rely on round robin reading—or the process of asking children to take turns reading a few sentences or paragraphs at a time—as their only oral reading strategy. Time and again, the problematic nature of round robin reading and its variants (e.g., popcorn, popsicle, and combat reading; e.g., Ash & Kuhn, 2006) has been discussed in the research literature. However, from our experience in classrooms and our conversations with teachers, we know that these "strategies" are still used by teachers who genuinely don't know what else to do.

---

[1]Throughout this book, we use the term *text* to refer to written materials comprised of connected sentences, such as those found in books, newspapers, poetry, and other reading materials. It should not be confused with the term *textbook,* although texts from children's textbooks can also be used.

We provide two approaches to oral reading instruction that are easy to implement, effective, and seen by both teachers and learners as an enjoyable component of their literacy curriculum. These approaches, Fluency-Oriented Reading Instruction (FORI) and Wide Reading Instruction, are useful alternatives to round robin reading and its equivalents.

The two approaches presented in this book are ideal for either whole-class literacy instruction or, alternatively, for groups of students who are in the process of becoming fluent readers. They incorporate an approach to using a shared text, be it a selection from a basal reader or literature anthology or a trade book, which allows your students to use challenging material with significant amounts of support. However, the approaches differ in the number of texts that they use, with the FORI approach incorporating a greater degree of repetition than the Wide Reading approach. In fact, FORI makes use of a single challenging text over the course of the week and incorporates echo, choral, and partner reading of that text into the weekly lesson plan. (See Chapter 2 for the weekly lesson plans that compose the FORI as well as the Wide Reading approach.) Wide Reading, on the other hand, uses three texts, rather than one (suggestions for creating class sets to texts without purchasing large numbers of books are also explored in Chapter 2), and makes more consistent use of echo reading. However, despite these differences, various studies have shown that both FORI and Wide Reading lead to significant gains in the literacy development of the students using these approaches.

HOW DO WE KNOW IT WORKS?

We have spent the past 5 years examining these approaches in the classroom as part of a large-scale, federally funded (Interagency Education Research Initiative–National Science Foundation–National Institute of Child Health and Human Development) research project designed to investigate the development of fluent reading in second grade. The project took place in a large number of classrooms with teachers working to encourage the development of fluency in their students. The children in these classrooms lived in a broad range of communities—urban, rural, and suburban (in New Jersey, Georgia, Illinois, Kansas, and California)—and had a broad range of economic backgrounds. Our research indicated that the approaches are effective for all these learners if you adhere to certain key principles:

- *Bring comprehension to the fore.* By concentrating on the texts' meaning early in the lesson, students develop the insight that comprehension, rather than simply word recognition, is the ultimate purpose of reading (Hoffman & Crone, 1985).

- *Select material that is challenging* (e.g., grade level or above). Students who are experiencing difficulties with their reading development are often given texts that are several levels below their peers. Although it is important that students read material at their independent level, supported reading of challenging texts allows them to expand their word recognition knowledge and develop their fluency while introducing them to a wider range of concepts than they would likely encounter with less complex texts.
- *Provide them with appropriate levels of scaffolding* (Kuhn et al., 2006; Stahl & Heubach, 2005). Because students become frustrated when attempting to read challenging material on their own, it is critical that they receive support, or scaffolding, through strategies such as those outlined in this book.
- *Make sure your students spend significant amounts of time—at least 20 minutes a day—reading connected text as part of this approach.* This principle underscores the others. Without ample opportunities to practice what they are learning about reading, your students will never develop the comfort with print that is necessary for them to become fluent readers.

We discuss how these principles are integrated into two cohesive approaches throughout the upcoming chapters.

IS REPETITION THE KEY?

One element that most fluency strategies have in common is their use of repetition (Samuels, 2006). In fact, repeated reading of connected text has been considered essential to successful fluency instruction (e.g., Rasinski, 1989) and has been proven effective in improving automaticity and prosody in dozens of research studies (Dowhower, 1989; National Reading Panel, 2000). However, a recent review (Kuhn & Stahl, 2003) found that there was little difference in student achievement when repeated reading strategies were compared with the nonrepeated reading of a wide range of texts with appropriate support—an idea we wanted to explore further.

In order to do this, we designed lesson plans with a fluency focus that were easy to implement and appropriate for second and (in many cases) third grades. We considered these two types of instruction, one based upon repeated reading and the other based on the wide reading of equivalent amounts of text, in real classrooms in order to determine how well the students learned using these different approaches. We compared these approaches with other methods of reading instruction, such as guided reading and reading workshop, through a series of assessments that evaluated students' comprehension development as well as how quickly and accurately they read both connected text and word lists. As a result, we feel confident recommending both approaches as the basis of your shared reading program for second and third graders (the approaches are explained in detail in Chapter 2).

We feel that these approaches are successful in helping students become fluent readers because they ensure that students have extensive opportunities to read challenging books aloud with appropriate scaffolding. These approaches provide learners with the opportunity to practice—in context—what they are learning about literacy, pulling together their knowledge of word recognition and allowing them to become accurate and automatic readers. Additionally, the modeling helps students learn to apply expression to their own reading, allowing them to sound like skilled readers. Finally, the fact that students experience success through these approaches serves to further motivate their learning.

Although we would not suggest that these approaches serve as the only components of your classroom's reading instruction (we would certainly include writing, word work, and other strategy instruction as part of a balanced approach to literacy development), we do consider them to be highly effective in developing students' reading fluency. As such, they can serve as the frame within which your whole-class reading instruction is built.

In order to help you understand both of these approaches as a whole as well as the elements that contribute to their effective use in the classroom, we have organized the book accordingly:

In Chapter 1, we discuss why fluency is important along with its role in learning to read.

In Chapter 2, we describe the weekly programs and the research behind them.

In Chapter 3, we present ways to carry out partner, choral, and echo reading, key scaffolding strategies in the approaches we recommend.

In Chapter 4, we explain how to weave comprehension into our fluency instruction.

In Chapter 5, we explore ways to develop motivation within fluency instruction.

In Chapter 6, we discuss strategies that lay the groundwork for fluency development in struggling readers.

In Chapter 7, we discuss how caregivers can be involved in their children's fluency development.

In Chapter 8, we describe formal and informal assessments for oral reading and fluency development.

In Chapter 9, we discuss an alternative approach to text selection for fluency instruction.

We have also prepared a glossary of critical terms, found at the end of the book for your easy reference. Each chapter's critical terms are identified in *italics*.

The contributors to this book were all part of the team of researchers that investigated reading fluency as part of the Interagency Education Research Initiative study. Each of us has several years of experience as researchers of reading fluency as well as in listening to hundreds of children learning to read fluently. Several of us also have extensive experience as teachers of reading fluency. Thus, we have presented joint perspectives from state-of-the art theory and scientific evidence along with grounded classroom perspectives on reading fluency. As such, we hope that this book will make a positive contribution to your reading curriculum by expanding your repertoire in terms of effective approaches to literacy instruction.

REFERENCES

Ash, G. E., & Kuhn, M. R. (2006). Meaningful oral and silent reading in the elementary and middle school classroom: Breaking the round robin reading addiction. In T. Rasinski, C. Blachowicz, & K. Lems (Eds.), *Fluency instruction: Research-based best practices* (pp. 155–172). New York: Guilford Press.

Dowhower, S. (1989). Repeated reading: Theory into practice. *The Reading Teacher, 42*, 502–507.

Hoffman, J. V., & Crone, S. (1985). The oral recitation lesson: A research-derived strategy for reading basal texts. In J. A. Niles & R. V. Lalik (Eds.), *Issues in literacy: A research perspective* (34th yearbook of the National Reading Conference, pp. 76–83). Rochester, NY: National Reading Conference.

Kuhn, M. R., Schwanenflugel, P. J., Morris, R. D., Morrow, L. M., Woo, D., et al. (2006). Teaching children to become fluent and automatic readers. *Journal of Literacy Research, 38*, 357–387.

Kuhn, M. R., & Stahl, S. A. (2003). Fluency: A review of developmental and remedial practices. *Journal of Educational Psychology, 95*, 3–22.

National Reading Panel. (2000). *Report of the subgroups: National Reading Panel.* Washington, DC: National Institute of Child Health and Human Development.

Rasinski, T. V. (1989). Fluency for everyone: Incorporating fluency instruction in the classroom. *The Reading Teacher, 42*, 690–693.

Samuels, S. J. (2006). Reading fluency: Its past, present, and future. In T. Rasinski, C. Blachowicz, & K. Lems (Eds.), *Fluency instruction: Research-based best practices* (pp. 7–20). New York: Guilford Press.

Stahl, S. A., & Heubach, K. (2005). Fluency-oriented reading instruction. *Journal of Literacy Research, 37*, 25–60.

Acknowledgments

We thank the many research assistants who have worked on the research reported in this book: Stephanie Beane, Tara Benton, Ashley Buckley, Whitney Cook, Erin Dowty, Trish Foels, Rebecca Gara, Annmarie Hamilton, Karen Hickland, Soyoung Kim, Pat Janes, Samantha Johnson, Emily Moore, Hye Pae, Susan Parault, Jessie Powers, Hilary Ruston, Jan Sieczko, Claire Smith, Gregory Strauss, Wanda Swigget, and Franklin Turner, and administrative assistants Cathy Frosh, Lisa Iorillo, Shea Ray, and Marta Zurbriggen. We thank the following advisors for their technical help and advice: Arnie Glass, Scott Paris, Joe Wisenbaker, Greg Palardy, Tim Rasinski, Sean Hendricks, and Marilyn Adams. We also thank Natalie Graham, Chris Jennison, and Anna Nelson at The Guilford Press for leading this book through the editorial process and into print. This research was supported in part by the Interagency Education Research Initiative, a program of research jointly managed by the National Science Foundation (Grant No. 0089258), the Institute of Education Sciences in the U.S. Department of Education, and the National Institute of Child Health and Human Development in the National Institutes of Health (National Institutes of Health Grant No. 7 R01 HD040746-06).

Contents

FLUENCY IN THE CLASSROOM

CHAPTER 1

Becoming a Fluent Reader
From Theory to Practice

PAULA J. SCHWANENFLUGEL and HILARY P. RUSTON

THIS CHAPTER DISCUSSES:

- Definitions of reading fluency.
- The issue of word callers.
- How fluency develops in readers.
- Oral versus silent reading.
- When fluency instruction is appropriate.

Learning to read fluently is an important goal for elementary school children. We are concerned, as no doubt you are, about children who cannot read fluently—often despite considerable instruction—for these are the children for whom reading never quiet seems to "click" and for whom reading remains an uncomfortable, arduous toil. We rightly worry that these children may have serious difficulty both comprehending and learning from text, and that they will never really enjoy reading for its own sake or for the rich rewards that reading brings. It is therefore important to determine early on whether a learner has a fluency problem because this may be a preliminary sign of a cascading set of complications ahead.

If you are reading this book, you are probably a member of the growing choruses of teachers who have pinpointed reading fluency as an instructional concern for your classroom. Our goal for this chapter is to provide you with both an understanding of what reading fluency consists of and a rationale for placing increased focus on activities devoted to reading fluency in your classroom. We also present the research base that we hope will answer some of the questions that we have been asked regarding the nature of reading fluency over the years.

WHAT EXACTLY IS READING FLUENCY?

If you are confused about the meaning of the term *reading fluency*, you are not alone. A number of definitions of reading fluency in both the research and popular literature seem, at times, to conflict with each other. However, we would argue that this conflict is based more on the details of the definitions than on any inherent substance in them. Few researchers would argue that reading fluency is a single skill. Rather, it is the orchestration of a number of subskills, which, taken together, comprise reading fluency. The debate regarding the definition of reading fluency is more about which skills are important to this definition rather than what fluent reading ultimately "looks like" in practice.

Some of the proposed component skills that contribute to reading fluently can be found in Figure 1.1. We use solid arrows to indicate skills that most researchers agree are central to reading fluency, whereas the dashed arrows point to skills that are somewhat more controversial. However, regardless of the agreement or disagreement over the relationship to reading fluency, virtually all researchers in this area would agree with the fol-

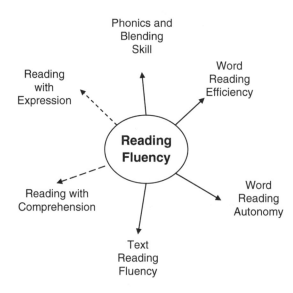

FIGURE 1.1. Skills underlying the development of fluent reading (solid arrow = generally agreed upon; dashed arrow = somewhat less agreed upon).

lowing statement: Fluent readers can read quickly and accurately, with basic comprehension and expression that reflects the grammar of the sentence.

Let's take a clockwise tour around this diagram. Beginning at the top, for a child to be a fluent reader, he or she must be able to quickly identify letters, and perhaps larger units such as syllables, prefixes, and suffixes, and translate them into speech (Coltheart & Leahy, 1992; Treiman, Goswami, & Bruck, 1990; Wolf, Bowers, & Biddle, 2000). For simplicity, we will call this skill *phonics and blending*. This skill, by itself, does not lead to fluent reading, but without it there is little hope that a child will be able to read new words quickly. With practice, some highly frequent words, suffixes, and multiletter phonics patterns eventually undergo a process called *unitization*, in which the letter patterns come to be processed holistically rather than as slow, sequential phonics patterns (Cunningham, Healy, Kanengiser, Chizzick, & Willitts, 1988; Ehri, 1995). To illustrate, try to count how many *t*'s you find in the following passage, from Cunningham et al., while you read the passage straight through:

> Up in the sky, Mother and Father Bird flew up in the clouds. Now the spring was here and they were looking for a new home. Below them they saw a wonderful place in the woods. When the birds landed, they began making their new home. All day long they worked very hard. Mother Bird ruffled her feathers. She and Father Bird were so happy there. New in their home they had six small blue eggs. She gathered them close so they could be warm. In only another week, the new babies would be there.

How many did *t*'s you find? You could have found 25 of them. However, most people miss several of the *t*'s in the word *the*. If that happened to you, it is because you have ceased to process familiar words such as *the* as a series of letters. Instead, you have come to process the word *the* as a whole and now have difficulty distinguishing the parts from that whole. Similarly, as children gain reading skill, they actually become *worse* at detecting the letter *t* in words such as *the* (Cunningham et al., 1988).

Moving along this diagram, we find the skill of *word reading efficiency*, which requires the quick and accurate word reading skills that we consider the sine qua non of skilled reading in the early stages (Adams, 1990; Stanovich, 1990). It is possibly *the* key bottleneck on the way to fluent reading (Lyon, 1995). Children make enormous strides in this skill during the early elementary school years but gradually level off toward the end of elementary school and into middle school as this skill reaches its maximum. However, word reading fluency distinguishes skilled from less skilled readers in a manner that is remarkably stable throughout elementary school and adulthood (Juel, 1988).

Moving further, we find *word reading autonomy*. This term refers to the fact that, at some point in the process of becoming a fluent reader, children simply cannot help but process print, even when they would rather avoid doing so. Therefore, skilled readers find themselves reading text on the bottom of the CNN news program even when they would rather not read it! This *automaticity* aspect can be seen in Figure 1.2. Try naming the pictures without reading their associated print. Do you find that you have to read the words anyway? It's hard to avoid them. Obviously, we have contrived the situation so you can actually feel the effects of automaticity. Normally, however, this word reading automaticity is helpful to us because it orients our attention to the print.

Moving down Figure 1.1, we come to *text reading fluency*. This term refers to what most people think of when they think of fluent reading. Fluent readers can read *connected text* quickly and accurately. This skill seems to emerge once children have achieved word reading fluency. Texts provide grammatical features, plot, and organization that help us comprehend what we are reading. With fluent text reading, a child can take advantage of the repetitious nature and predictability of text.

In some definitions of reading fluency, *reading with expression* takes a front seat as a hallmark of fluent reading (Kuhn & Stahl, 2003; Rasinski, 2004; Zutell & Rasinski, 1991). The controversy over this skill is not so much a question of whether fluent readers read with expression, because most fluent readers do. Instead, the issue is the role that expressiveness or *reading prosody* plays in fluency. Read the following sentences aloud:

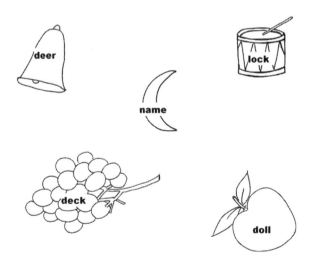

FIGURE 1.2. Automatic word reading: Name the pictures without reading the print on each picture. You should notice that this is difficult.

A tall, thin, smiling man came walking from the house. Jan and Julie went to meet him. He could see them looking at his garden. "Would you like to see my garden?" he asked.

Expressiveness refers to the pauses and stress as well as the rise-and-fall patterns of spoken language. You may or may not have paused at each comma in the first sentence. Some adults do and some do not. You probably heard the pitch of your voice course downward and pause briefly when you came to the word *house* in the first sentence. You probably heard your voice rise at the question mark after *garden*. Yes–no questions (i.e., questions that can be answered with a simple "yes" or "no") seem to require this tonal rise, though who, what, when, and where questions may not (Miller & Schwanenflugel, 2006).

Some think that this expressiveness may provide feedback that children can use for comprehension (Kuhn & Stahl, 2003). In our own research, we have found that good reading prosody is an indicator of a child who has fast and accurate word and text reading skills (Schwanenflugel, Hamilton, Kuhn, Wisenbaker, & Stahl, 2004). By itself, general expressiveness may not tell us all that much about whether a child has good reading comprehension. We have found that expressiveness is a relevant indicator of good comprehension only when children read grammatically complex sentences (Miller & Schwanenflugel, 2006). Even then, changes in pitch seem to be more relevant for comprehension than are pauses. Word and text reading fluency are better indicators of good comprehension, at least in early elementary school. But if a child is reading with expression, you can be sure he or she has achieved reading fluency.

Finally, going back to Figure 1.1, we come upon *reading with comprehension*. Some definitions of reading fluency put reading comprehension up front and center (Fuchs, Fuchs, Hosp, & Jenkins, 2003; Wolf & Katzir-Cohen, 2001), the belief being that children cannot be deemed *fluent* if they do not understand what they are reading. Including reading with comprehension in this definition means that reading fluency is conceived as *rate-limited comprehension*, which is reading quickly while still understanding what is being read. It is important to recognize that if you merely speed read through a passage without understanding it, you would not want to call that fluent reading. Individuals who do this are sometimes referred to as *word callers*—that is, children who can read quickly and accurately but do not understand much of what they have read. (We address this issue below.)

Our view is that reading fluency is a bridge to comprehension, but only one of several. Other factors such as vocabulary, world knowledge, inference abilities, etc., are important to comprehension as well. Toward the end of elementary school, most children are sufficiently fluent to move through texts quickly and easily, and fluency is no longer an important basis of poor comprehension (Schwanenflugel, Meisinger, Wisenbaker, Kuhn, & Morris, 2005). For them, most comprehension problems do not come from the fluency part of the comprehension equation. There are, however, slow readers in middle and high school who have fluency issues that affect comprehension (Rasinski, Padak, McKeon, Wilfong, Friedauer, & Heim, 2005). These are likely to be teenagers for whom reading has been a struggle all along. Basically, without specific work on fluency, comprehension is unlikely to improve for these older readers. However, even fluent readers may have difficulty comprehending. So we would rather acknowledge the central role of reading fluency to comprehension without muddying the waters by including good reading comprehension as an *essential* ingredient of fluency.

WORD CALLERS, WORD CALLERS: WHERE ARE YOU?

One of the comments that we hear, with amazing regularity, from teachers and other researchers is that reading fluency is not important because it creates children who are mere *word callers*; learners who do not understand what they are reading even though they can "read" well. We get asked, "Isn't all this emphasis on reading fluency grossly misplaced? Can't children compensate for their poor reading fluency by using guessing strategies and world knowledge to help them understand?" We would be more sympathetic to the implied message in these questions if, indeed, there were a lot of word callers out there. In fact, in our research on reading fluency in second and third grade children, we have found very few of them. How do we know this?

First, we need to define what we think people really mean when they use the term *word caller*. We think it means that there are children in classrooms who are sometimes more fluent at reading certain passages than they are at comprehending them. So these children can read the words from their grade-level text just fine, but still do not understand what they read after they have read it.

To get at this idea of word calling, we tested children on their reading fluency and their comprehension. We used national standardized tests of word reading fluency, text reading fluency, and reading comprehension abilities to tell us which children had good reading fluency and which had good comprehension skills compared to his or her age-mates (Meisinger & Bradley, 2006). Presumably, the word calling hypothesis would state that many children who scored well on tests of word and text fluency (let's use a standard score of 110[1]) would score comparatively poorly on reading com-

---

[1]These numbers refer to a test with a national average of 100; children who score 15 points below the national average are considered to be at considerable risk.

prehension tests (let's use a standard score of 90 or lower). Of the over 1,500 second, 300 third, and 100 fifth graders we tested, we have found a very low rate of word calling by this definition. Only 1% of second and third graders and only 3% of fifth graders would qualify. Moreover, when we asked teachers to nominate children in their classrooms whom they believed might qualify as word callers, we found that they often selected children who did not have good comprehension *or* reading fluency. In other words, teachers often nominated your *garden variety* basic poor readers (Stanovich, 1988) as word callers. So, in one way, teachers were absolutely right in thinking that the children were not skilled readers. They just did not fit the definition of a true word caller. Thus, although word callers certainly do exist, they do not seem to be all that common, at least in the early elementary school years.

In sum, we don't feel that we should focus our concerns about reading fluency and fluency-oriented reading practices on the possibility of creating word callers. Instead, it seems much more likely that carrying out activities in your classrooms to help children improve reading fluency will improve their comprehension most of the time as well, especially if you emphasize comprehension and appropriate speed and expression (as opposed to speed for speed's sake).

HOW DOES FLUENCY DEVELOP?

Reading fluency develops through *practice*. With practice a child moves from being a hesitant, word-by-word reader who reads with considerable difficulty to a fluent, expressive, automatic reader who understands what he or she reads. Like other skills, such as playing the violin or performing routines on the balance beam, learning to read fluently takes practice. Like other new skills, when you practice something that has a bit of challenge to it, you get quicker and more accurate. Like any skill, it does not help much to practice something you can already do quite well. It also does not make any sense to practice something for which you are not yet remotely ready. Instead, you need to find a level that allows you to improve (Ericsson, Krampe, & Tesch-Römer, 1993). It also helps to carry out this practice with feedback from a teacher, family member, or friend who can read well enough (Ericsson et al., 1993).

These rules of thumb have a number of substantiated educational reasons behind them. First, we tend to be motivated by challenges that are just a bit beyond our immediate grasp (Moneta & Csikszentmihalyi, 1999). Second, our attention is drawn to novel challenges, and we concentrate better on them (Berlyne, 1954; McCall, Kennedy, & Appelbaum, 1977). By reading extensively, we expose ourselves to new words and ideas and repeat some old words and ideas. Through this method, we gain automaticity for the old words and phrases and lay down new memory traces for the new ones (Logan, 1997). Finally, by receiving feedback on our performance, we make sure that we are not practicing incorrectly—something that would hamper our future performance.

Figure 1.3 illustrates the role of practice in four children. When children become more fluent, they increase the number of correct words they read per minute, as was noted above. The graph shows the passage reading times for a minute of reading by children we will call Sierra, Colt, Javier, and Linda. These children were practicing the same passage in their classrooms at least once a day during the week.

On Monday, Sierra was already incredibly quick and accurate in her reading of the passage. She did not gain much fluency over the week. She probably could have been given a more difficult passage to work on—something that would have allowed her to improve her reading.

In contrast, Javier and Colt were similarly slow on the passage on Monday, and they continued to mirror each other in that, by the end of the week, the benefits they received from practice had leveled off. This leveling off demonstrates a typical *power law of practice*, or a diminishing-returns effect that occurs with practice (Logan, 1992). This passage was just right for them and, by the end of the week, they had had enough practice, and more practice probably would not help much. It was time to move on to something else.

Unfortunately, the passage was much too difficult for Linda, and, quite possibly, she had not yet mastered enough of the basic decoding principles to get much out of this type of reading practice. As a result, she began the week by reading incredibly slowly and inaccurately and ended

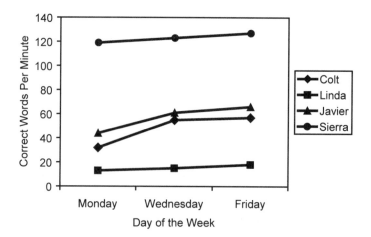

FIGURE 1.3. The progress of four children, in correct words per minute, who practiced the same passage every day for a week.

the week the same way. She would have experienced a greater benefit from practice on something else, possibly an easier passage or perhaps a different type of instruction altogether (see Chapter 5 for instructional approaches with struggling readers).

As any elite musician or gymnast will tell you, poor practice is sometimes worse than no practice at all; bad habits can be picked up that need to be unlearned later (Siegler & Shipley, 1995). We believe that much the same is true in learning to read. That is why we stress reading with a knowledgeable other or a model that can demonstrate correct reading. This model can present either the correct way to read a word or passage or provide immediate corrective feedback, thereby assisting the child to make the most of reading practice. We see little point in sitting children down with a book they can barely read and assuming that, if they just work at it hard enough, they will become fluent readers. You wouldn't expect this kind of reading accomplishment any more than you would expect a young gymnast to start off with a full twisting double back flip.

There is one caveat to this point, however. When children are highly motivated, they can often read text that might otherwise be too difficult for them, as the recent Harry Potter phenomenon indicated. If children really want to read a particular text, it may be beneficial to allow them to try to read it. If they find it too difficult, you may want to create a tape-recorded version they can use as a model or ask a parent or volunteer to partner read these items with the children. I (P.S.) recollect with great fondness how delighted my boys were that their awesome father was pleased to partner-read the entire Harry Potter series with them! And, yes, they did gain fluency from all those thousands of pages of partner reading (not to mention lots of warm and wonderful shared family memories around the books)!

IS ALL PRACTICE ALIKE? SHOULD I EMPHASIZE ORAL READING OR SILENT READING IN MY CLASSROOM?

In our experience with teachers, we have found that virtually all of them rightly believe that "practice makes perfect" when it comes to developing reading fluency. However, they are often confused about how best to carry out that practice. Among the questions they ask is whether or not they should emphasize oral reading or lots of silent reading in their classroom.

This turns out to be a complex question. The National Reading Panel (NRP) (National Institute of Child Health and Human Development, 2000) published a review of experimental studies that examined the role of sustained silent reading (SSR) on children's fluency development and reading achievement and concluded, "the NRP did not find evidence supporting the effectiveness of encouraging independent silent reading as a means of improving reading achievement" (pp. 3–4). This conclusion basically shocked the reading community. SSR time during the school day had become a commonplace and protected activity in U.S. schools. SSR time allowed every child to read books he or she wanted to read. Teachers wanted to preserve that special time in their classroom. The research results seemed to fly in the face of reason.

So what does research say about the relative effectiveness of oral as compared to silent reading? Research suggests that it may depend on the reading skills of the children. For less-skilled readers, oral reading may be better. There's a tendency for low-skilled readers to understand what they are reading better with oral reading than silent reading (Fuchs, Fuchs, & Maxwell, 1988; Holmes & Allison, 1985; Miller & Smith, 1985, 1990; Mullikin, Henk, & Fortner, 1992; Swalm, 1972). Results are mixed for other children or adults. Some studies suggest that perhaps it does not matter, whereas others find that comprehension during oral reading is better (McCallum, Sharp, Bell, & George, 2004; Mullikin et al., 1992; Salasoo, 1986). Either way, it seems that perhaps we are safer to emphasize oral reading in early elementary school classrooms.

Why does oral reading work? One view that we favor is that oral reading helps children process information in the text. Oral reading may ensure that children do not skip over difficult words while reading the text (Juel & Holmes, 1981) and may boost the *phonological memory code* (i.e., the little voice in your head) that we use to keep information circling around while we put the words and message together (Gathercole & Baddeley, 1993). Indeed, adults seem to resort to switching to the oral reading mode when they encounter difficulty understanding what they are reading during the silent reading of texts (Hardyck & Petrinovich, 1970).

Another distinct view is that oral reading may support the movement from the social origins of reading to the internalization of the reading process itself (Prior & Welling, 2001). The idea is that, when children are young, they are read to aloud by a caring adult, usually the parent, and the social features of reading take precedence. Indeed, we know that positive interactions during these early reading experiences seem to provide the kind of support that fosters the development of reading (Bus & van IJzendoorn, 1992). Children who are read to frequently by a caring adult who shares ideas and provides enjoyment during these times tend to be those who are skilled readers later. Upon receiving formal reading instruction, the child begins to take over responsibility for the reading by reading aloud with assistance from a supportive adult, often the teacher. Once the child has achieved some level of decoding speed and accuracy, he or she is ready to read independently, but may still need the external self-regulating function that reading aloud provides to support comprehension. Finally, at some point the child is able to read silently because he or she has internalized the reading process and is now self-regulating. The processes engaged by oral reading have moved "underground." This process of internalization in learning to read is represented in Figure 1.4.

This point brings us back to the issue of what to do about SSR time in the classroom. Research has documented a number of problems that teachers and children have with SSR time (Gambrell, 1978). One of the problems is that SSR assumes that children are equipped to read independently. Some students simply cannot read independently yet without a lot of decoding assistance. Beginning readers tend to select books that are too difficult for them (Donovan, Smolkin, & Lomax, 2000). Other children may have quite a bit of difficulty staying on task during SSR time; they may have general behavioral difficulties that keep them from making the best use of this time (Bryan, Fawson, & Reutzel, 2003; Lee-Daniels & Murray, 2000); or they may find it boring to engage in the same routine day after day after day. Most of these problems have a solution, though, and some of these are discussed below. On the other hand, there are definite advantages to SSR because it allows children to choose what they read. It is well established that having the authority to choose what they read is highly motivating for children (Gambrell, 1996), particularly when they have a goal for that reading (Guthrie & Cox, 2001), such as sharing a review with other students or learning more about a certain topic that interests them.

If you still want to preserve SSR in your classroom because of this element of *choice*, we can appreciate that decision. Furthermore, there are a number of things you could do that would help fix some of the problems associated with SSR. For example, you could try having children "mumble read" (Kragler, 1995) instead. Mumble reading is exactly what it sounds like—every child chooses a book that he or she wants to read, but reads it aloud to him- or herself by softly mumbling the text. You could practice mumble reading with the children so they learn just how loud they can read without a combined effect of group reading that disturbs the whole building!

| Adult reads aloud to child. | Child reads aloud to adult. | Child reads aloud alone. | Child reads quietly alone. |

FIGURE 1.4. The process of internalizing oral reading from a Vygotskian framework.

Another solution for the problems of SSR time might be to use taped stories with headphones, or reading while listening, for children who are not quite ready to read independently. Kuhn and Stahl (2003) reported that evidence is somewhat mixed for the use of these taped stories, however. It seems this procedure works best when children are held responsible for the reading. They should practice their reading along with the tape and complete a running record for the teacher or read the book aloud to a classroom neighbor or younger student. They can also share what they think about a particular text, or write some sort of response for it. Because some students have difficulty following along, it is also possible to insert little "dings" that tell children when to turn the page. This technique allows the children to deal with the mechanics of tracking their reading along with tapes. However, this addition is not necessary for all learners. The reading-while-listening approach also seems to work best when the texts are challenging but do not greatly exceed the children's current reading level. Teachers may need to help children identify appropriate texts and screen out books that are too advanced for this form of scaffolded reading.

Although there may seem to be too many "ifs" to successfully carry out SSR as a whole-class activity, we think that these alternatives can increase the engagement of your students during independent reading time. We also hope that we have convinced you that there are a number of good reasons to focus on oral reading in the classroom. As other authors in this book attest, there are a number of effective ways to carry out extensive oral reading that provide *scaffolding* for student learning. The important concern is to ensure that the children are processing lots and lots of text and are provided with the much-needed practice that SSR was designed to achieve. We favor the idea of rethinking the acronym SSR from meaning *sustained silent reading* to *self-selected reading* instead (Reutzel & Cooper, 2000). In our classrooms we emphasize lots of extended oral reading practice for children who are still achieving fluency.

WHICH CHILDREN NEED
FLUENCY-ORIENTED INSTRUCTION?

In a balanced reading program, there is a time and a place for the curriculum to provide different types of instruction, given the developmental needs of the young readers. The striking resemblance among many developmental models of reading (e.g., Chall, 1996) indicates that, in the early phases of learning to read, children first formulate ideas about the form and function of print. Before they can actually read, they learn about the sound system of language (called *phonological awareness*), whereby they come to appreciate and enjoy rhyme and alliteration. They also build basic vocabulary and world knowledge that they will use later to form the meaning basis for reading. Children who are building this basic sound, meaning, and print knowledge are usually in preschool and kindergarten, but these systems continue to be refined throughout elementary school. Fluency-oriented instruction is obviously not developmentally appropriate during this period.

In the next phase, children learn to connect individual letters and groups of letters to speech sounds and word meanings acquired in preschool (Adams, 1990). That is, they learn to connect sounds to print and to blend these sounds together to form words that have meanings. During this phase, they are spending a lot of their cognitive resources merely figuring out what the text actually says. Children may be starting the work of building fluency, but it is not the main focus here. During this phase, which usually occurs toward the end of kindergarten and throughout first grade, whole-classroom emphasis on fluency is probably not appropriate, although small-group emphasis may be appropriate for advanced children.

Once children have established a set of *sight words* that they can read readily and are able to decode most of the words that they find in text, they are ready to receive fluency instruction. For most children, this phase occurs toward the end of first grade and throughout second and third grades as they confirm these skills through practice. There is a time for everything, and the time for fluency-oriented instruction is *after* children have developed their basic decoding ability.

Once children have achieved fluent reading, it is important to move the focus to other issues, such as comprehension instruction. We become concerned, for example, when we see a fifth-grade classroom with a misplaced instructional *persistence* on phonological awareness, phonics, and single sight-word instruction when the children have long since established these basic skills. Similarly, we would think that an emphasis on fluency-oriented instruction past third grade would need some special sort of rationale.

What might such special situations be? If, for example, your older elementary or middle school classroom contained an unusual number of struggling readers who are only just beginning to establish fluency, an emphasis on fluency would be highly appropriate. If you had an older elementary or middle school child who seemed to comprehend grade-level texts well but his or her oral reading skills still seemed unusually slow and inaccurate, there may be some justification for emphasizing fluency. We worry that, as the reading demands of school increase, the child's slow reading will frustrate and hamper his or her ability to complete the amount of reading materials needed to be successful in school. In such a case, we would recommend some emphasis on fluency instruction using complex materials. This way, the child would continue to acquire vocabulary and comprehension skills commensurate with his or her cognitive skills and important for advanced texts, while still obtaining the fluency instruction he or she needs.

No matter what the age of the students, however, it is important (1) to emphasize that comprehension is the ultimate goal of reading and (2) to teach a range of literacy activities that support this goal. After all, fluency is just the bridge on our way to comprehension and enjoyment of the printed word. It is not our ultimate destination.

REFERENCES

Adams, M. J. (1990). *Beginning to read: Thinking and learning about print*. Cambridge, MA: MIT Press.

Berlyne, D. (1954). A theory of human curiosity. *British Journal of Psychology, 39*, 184–185.

Bryan, G., Fawson, P. C., & Reutzel, D. R. (2003). Sustained silent reading: Exploring the value of literature discussion with three non-engaged readers. *Reading Research and Instruction, 43*, 47–73.

Bus, A. G., & van IJzendoorn, M. H. (1992). Patterns of attachment in frequently and infrequently reading mother–child dyads. *Journal of Genetic Psychology, 153*, 395–403.

Chall, J. S. (1996). *Learning to read: The great debate*. Fort Worth, TX: Harcourt Brace.

Coltheart, V., & Leahy, J. (1992). Children's and adults' reading of nonwords: Effects of regularity and consistency. *Journal of Experimental Psychology: Learning, Memory, and Cognition, 18*, 718–729.

Cunningham, T. F., Healy, A. F., Kanengiser, N., Chizzick, L., & Willitts, R. L. (1988). Investigating the boundaries of reading units across ages and reading levels. *Journal of Experimental Child Psychology, 45*, 175–208.

Donovan, C. A., Smolkin, L. B., & Lomax, R. G. (2000). Beyond the independent-level text: Considering the reader–text match in first graders' self-selections during recreational reading. *Reading Psychology, 21*, 309–333.

Ehri, L. C. (1995). Phases of development in learning to read words by sight. *Journal of Research in Reading, 18*, 116–125.

Ericsson, K. A., Krampe, R. T., & Tesch-Römer, C. (1993). The role of deliberate practice in the acquisition of expert performance. *Psychological Review, 100*, 363–406.

Fuchs, L. S., Fuchs, D., Hosp, M. K., & Jenkins, J. R. (2003). Oral reading fluency as an indicator of reading competence: A theoretical, empirical, and historical analysis. *Scientific Studies of Reading, 5*, 239–256.

Fuchs, L. S., Fuchs, D., & Maxwell, L. (1988).The validity of informal reading comprehension measures. *RASE: Remedial and Special Education, 9*, 20–28.

Gambrell, L. B. (1978). Getting started with sustained silent reading and keeping it going. *The Reading Teacher, 32*, 328–331.

Gambrell, L. B. (1996). Creating classroom cultures that foster reading motivation. *The Reading Teacher, 50*, 14–25.

Gathercole, S. E., & Baddeley, A. D. (1993). Phonological working memory: A critical building block for reading development and vocabulary acquisition? *European Journal of Psychology of Education, 8*, 259–272.

Guthrie, J. T., & Cox, K. E. (2001). Classroom conditions for motivation and engagement in reading. *Educational Psychology Review, 13,* 283–302.

Hardyck, C. D., & Petrinovich, L. F. (1970). Subvocal speech and comprehension level as a function of the difficulty level of reading material. *Journal of Verbal Learning and Verbal Behavior, 9,* 647–652.

Holmes, B. C., & Allison, R. W. (1985). The effect of four modes of reading on children's reading comprehension. *Reading Research and Instruction, 25,* 9–20.

Juel, C. (1988). Learning to read and write: A longitudinal study of 54 children from first to fourth grades. *Journal of Educational Psychology, 80,* 437–447.

Juel, C., & Holmes, B. (1981). Oral and silent reading of sentences. *Reading Research Quarterly, 16,* 545–568.

Kragler, S. (1995). The transition from oral to silent reading. *Reading Psychology, 16,* 395–408.

Kuhn, M. R., & Stahl, S. A. (2003). Fluency: A review of developmental and remedial practices. *Journal of Educational Psychology, 95,* 3–21.

Lee-Daniels, S. L., & Murray, B. A. (2000). DEAR me: What does it take to get children reading? *The Reading Teacher, 54,* 54–55.

Logan, G. D. (1992). Shapes of reaction-time distributions and shapes of learning curves: A test of the instance theory of automaticity. *Journal of Experimental Psychology: Learning, Memory, and Cognition, 18*(5), 883–914.

Logan, G. D. (1997). Automaticity and reading: Perspectives from the instance theory of automatization. *Reading and Writing Quarterly: Overcoming Learning Difficulties, 13,* 123–146.

Lyon, G. R. (1995). Toward a definition of dyslexia. *Annals of Dyslexia, 45,* 3–27.

McCall, R. B., Kennedy, C. B., & Appelbaum, M. I. (1977). Magnitude of discrepancy and the distribution of attention in infants. *Child Development, 48,* 772–785.

McCallum, R. S., Sharp, S., Bell, S. M., & George, T. (2004). Silent versus oral reading comprehension and efficiency. *Psychology in the Schools, 4,* 241–246.

Meisinger, E., & Bradley, B. A. (2006). *The myth and reality of the word caller: Teachers' concepts of fluency and comprehension.* Presentation to the National Reading Conference, Los Angeles, CA.

Miller, J., & Schwanenflugel, P. J. (2006). Prosody of syntactically complex sentences in the oral reading of young children. *Journal of Educational Psychology, 98* 839–843.

Miller, S. D., & Smith, D. E. (1985). Differences in literal and inferential comprehension after reading orally and silently. *Journal of Educational Psychology, 77,* 341–348.

Miller, S. D., & Smith, D. E. (1990). Relations among oral reading, silent reading and listening comprehension of students at differing competency levels. *Reading Research and Instruction, 29,* 73–84.

Moneta, G. B., & Csikszentmihalyi, M. (1999). Models of concentration in natural environments: A comparative approach based on streams of experiential data. *Social Behavior and Personality, 27,* 603–638.

Mullikin, C. N., Henk, W. H., & Fortner, B. H. (1992). Effects of story versus play genres on the comprehension of high, average, and low-achieving junior high school readers. *Reading Psychology, 13,* 273–290.

National Institute of Child Health and Human Development. (2000). *Report of the National Reading Panel. Teaching children to read: An evidence-based assessment of the scientific research literature on reading and its implications for reading instruction* (NIH Publication No. 00-4769). Washington, DC: U.S. Government Printing Office.

Prior, S. M., & Welling, K. A. (2001). "Read in your head": A Vygotskian analysis of the transition from oral to silent reading. *Reading Psychology, 22,* 1–15.

Rasinski, T. V. (2004). Creating fluent readers. *Educational Leadership, 61,* 46–51.

Rasinski, T. V., Padak, N. D., McKeon, C. A., Wilfong, L. G., Friedauer, J. A., & Heim, P. (2005). Is reading fluency a key for successful high school reading? *Journal of Adolescent and Adult Literacy, 49,* 22–27.

Reutzel, D. R., & Cooper, R. B. (2000). *Teaching children to read: Putting the pieces together.* Upper Saddle River, NJ: Prentice Hall.

Salasoo, A. (1986). Cognitive processing in oral and silent reading comprehension. *Reading Research Quarterly, 21,* 59–69.

Schwanenflugel, P. J., Hamilton, A. M., Kuhn, M. R., Wisenbaker, J., & Stahl, S. A. (2004). Becoming a fluent reader: Reading skill and prosodic features in the oral reading of young readers. *Journal of Educational Psychology, 96,* 119–129.

Schwanenflugel, P. J., Meisinger, E., Wisenbaker, J., Kuhn, M. R., & Morris, R. D. (2005). *Becoming a fluent and automatic reader in the early elementary school years.* Unpublished manuscript, University of Georgia.

Siegler, R. S., & Shipley, C. (1995). Variation, selection, and cognitive change. In G. Halford & T. Simon (Eds.), *Developing cognitive competence: New approaches to process modeling* (pp. 31–76). Hillsdale, NJ: Erlbaum.

Stanovich, K. E. (1988). Explaining the differences between the dyslexic and the garden-variety poor reader: The phonological-core variable-difference model. *Journal of Learning Disabilities, 21,* 590–604.

Stanovich, K. E. (1990). Concepts in developmental theories of reading skill: Cognitive resources, automaticity, and modularity. *Developmental Review, 10,* 72–100.

Swalm, J. E. (1972). A comparison of oral reading, silent reading and listening comprehension. *Education, 92,* 111–115.

Treiman, R., Goswami, U., & Bruck, M. (1990). Not all nonwords are alike: Implications for reading development and theory. *Memory and Cognition, 13,* 357–364.

Wolf, M., Bowers, P., & Biddle, K. (2000). Naming-speed processes, timing, and reading: A conceptual review. *Journal of Learning Disabilities, 3 3,* 387–407.

Wolf, M., & Katzir-Cohen, T. (2001). Reading fluency and its intervention. *Scientific Studies of Reading, 5,* 211–229.

Zutell, J., & Rasinski, T. V. (1991). Training teachers to attend to their students' oral reading fluency. *Theory into Practice, 30,* 211–217.

CHAPTER 2

Fluency-Oriented Reading
Two Whole-Class Approaches

MELANIE R. KUHN and DEBORAH G. WOO

THIS CHAPTER INCLUDES:

- A description of Fluency-Oriented Reading Instruction.
- A description of Wide Reading Instruction.
- The history of oral reading in the U.S. public school system.

If you listen to readers at the beginning of second grade, you will probably find that their reading is fairly choppy and expressionless. However, by the end of the second grade and into the third, their reading starts to become *fluent*. This means that, in addition to accurate *decoding*, their word recognition becomes automatic and they begin to use appropriate expression and phrasing. This transition is important, not only in terms of what your students' reading sounds like; it is also critical in terms of their overall reading development because it provides a bridge between decoding and comprehension (Pikulski & Chard, 2005; Rasinski & Hoffman, 2003). As such, it is important that reading instruction during the second—and often the third—grade focus on helping students develop into fluent readers.

Despite the importance of fluency in becoming a skilled reader, it was not a focus of most reading curricula until recently (e.g., Allington, 1983;

National Reading Panel, 2000). This omission is partially due to the fact that many approaches for fluency instruction are designed either to help individual learners or pairs of readers (e.g., repeated reading, paired repeated reading) or to supplement a classroom's current literacy instruction, as opposed to serving as its primary focus (e.g., Readers' theatre, the fluency development lesson; Kuhn & Stahl, 2003). The purpose of this chapter is to discuss two scientifically based reading programs—Fluency-Oriented Reading Instruction (FORI) and Wide Reading Instruction (Kuhn et al., 2006)—that are designed to help learners make the transition from reading that is word by word and monotonous to reading that is fluid and expressive, and which are meant to be a central component of your literacy curricula.

APPROACHES TO FLUENCY INSTRUCTION

The approaches presented in this chapter integrate four instructional principles into two cohesive literacy curricula (Kuhn et al., 2006). First, both approaches provide learners with extensive opportunities to read connected text. Second, they incorporate sufficient support—or *scaffolding*—to allow readers to work with challenging reading materials (grade level or higher). Third, both approaches provide feedback and *modeling* that emphasize appropriate word recognition, phrasing, and expression. Importantly, however, the two approaches deal with fluency development in two distinct ways: One approach uses scaffolded repetition as the backbone of its instructional approach, whereas the other uses scaffolded reading with a more extensive range of texts. While current research indicates that the Wide Reading approach has an edge in helping learners' word recognition, both of these approaches, which are part of an easy-to-implement program designed for the *shared reading* component of your literacy curriculum, are effective at assisting learners in making the transition to fluency.

We worked with a total of 24 classrooms in two regions, one in the Northeast and one in the Southeast, for 1 school year. Nine classrooms used the Wide Reading approach, nine used the repeated reading approach (FORI), and six used their regular reading curricula. After analyzing the students' test scores, we found that students using both the Wide Reading and the FORI did better than their peers on both the comprehension measure and the word recognition measure (Kuhn et al., 2006). Further, the students using the Wide Reading approach also did better in terms of their reading rate (correct words per minute [cwpm]).

IDENTIFYING TEXTS

Before discussing these two reading approaches, we want to address one of our principles—the use of challenging texts—in detail, because it diverges quite significantly from the use of instructional-level text. When it comes to selecting your texts, it is critical to recognize the role they will play in the success of your lessons. Because you will be providing significant scaffolding as part of your lesson plans, it is *essential* that the material you select be appropriately challenging. As such, your students need to be reading from material that is *at least* at their grade level (e.g., second graders should be reading texts identified as levels J–P; Fountas & Pinnell, 1999). You should be able to find such texts in your school's basals or literature anthologies; alternatively, you can use trade books, providing that each child in the class has his or her own copy of a given title.

The structure and support of the FORI and Wide Reading approaches will help your students, even those reading below grade level, to read each week's material successfully by the end of that week's lessons. Over the course of the year, your children's independent reading skills will gradually improve as a result of the amount of time they spend reading *connected text*. There are several resources for determining reading levels, including Gunning's *Best Books for Beginning Readers* (1998) and *The Fountas and Pinnel Leveled Book List, K–8* (Fountas & Pinnel, 2005). For second grade, we would recommend starting the year using late-first-/early-second-grade material (e.g., guided reading level J and K) and proceeding through late second/early third grade by the year's end (e.g., guided reading levels O and P). For third grade, we would suggest starting with late-second-/early-third-grade material (e.g., guided reading level P) and finishing the year with late-third-/early-fourth-grade material (e.g., guided reading levels T and U). However, if your students are already reading at grade level, it is recommended that you use texts that are at the upper end of their reading level (two to three *Guided Reading* levels higher than their current instructional levels). Alternatively, you can use the leveling system that is in place in your own school or district, but we stress that you identify levels that will be challenging for your learners.

FLUENCY-ORIENTED READING INSTRUCTION

Our first instructional approach was designed in response to one district's mandate that their students be taught exclusively through the use of grade-level texts. This mandate was considered problematic by many of the district's teachers because a large percentage of their students were reading below grade level. As a result, the teachers and their colleagues at the local

FLUENCY DON'TS

As a field, we often see appropriate suggestions translate into ineffective practice—for example, taking in a procedure that has the potential to assist our students in their literacy development and turning it into an unhelpful approach to reading instruction. Unfortunately, this outcome often leads us to throw up our hands, say the new strategy doesn't work, and eliminate the underlying procedure along with the ineffective practice. We have already seen such practices cropping up under the heading "fluency instruction." We mention them here in the hopes of preventing their proliferation within the classroom.

1. *Don't focus on words alone.* Although it is important that students develop automaticity with alphabet and word recognition, the development of these skills are not synonymous with fluency. Rather, fluency involves the reading of connected text with accurate and automatic word recognition and appropriate use of expression and phrasing. In fact, learners can become skilled at word recognition in isolation, but will not necessarily be able to transfer this knowledge to their reading of connected text without *explicit instruction* in this area.

2. *Don't spend too little time on oral reading.* Sometimes teachers engage in activities that do not provide much fluency practice for individual children. For example, in certain cases, Readers' Theatre has been used as a surrogate for round robin reading. In these unfortunate circumstances, each student is assigned a line of text that he or she is responsible for reading aloud. To add insult to injury, 30 minutes out of the 40- to 50-minute period has been spent assigning each reader his or her part. Not only is this an example of ineffective classroom management, it defeats the purpose of scaffolded fluency instruction—having *all* of your students engage in 20–40 minutes of daily supported reading of connected text. For students to become skilled readers, they need significant opportunities to read—not just one line (or even one paragraph) for each of your reading blocks.

3. *Don't have students focus on different texts while partner reading.* Although this next example may seem astounding, we witnessed at least one teacher whose students were "partner reading" using different texts! Unless both of your students are using the same material, it will be impossible for them to assist one another in their reading, thereby defeating the purpose of providing partners in the first place. It is essential that students read from the same selection when they are partnering with one another.

4. *Don't forget to emphasize comprehension.* If you are working with groups, it is important to consider the ultimate purpose of reading: the construction of meaning. We have seen students who are able to accurately, but slowly, decode texts with high levels of comprehension reassigned to easier texts in the hope that their reading rate would improve. Instead, we would suggest using repeated readings for short, supplemental periods (say, 5–10 minutes per day, perhaps during independent reading or center time). This approach should assist students in increasing their reading rate while allowing them to work with the challenging texts they are capable of comprehending.

5. *Don't use texts that are too short or too easy.* Although decodable texts, short poems, and brief "little" books all serve important roles in the literacy curriculum, they do not provide readers with sufficient opportunity to develop fluency. It is essential that

students read extensive, challenging text, with support, if they are going to make the transition from purposeful, hesitant, and often inaccurate decoding to reading that is accurate, automatic, and sounds like speech.

6. *Don't pose fluency as a race.* Similarly, the goal of *fluent reading* is not to increase students' speed at the expense of their comprehension. Students sometimes develop the notion, especially when using repeated readings with short texts, that good reading is fast reading. They may want to race through such texts, without any consideration as to how they sound, to increase their number of correct words per minute. This practice can often be rectified through your demonstration of speed reading (your students will no doubt laugh at how silly you sound). You can follow this up by showing them how reading at a normal rate incorporates additional elements, such as appropriate phrasing and pausing, and explain that becoming a fluent reader does not mean that you are participating in a race.

7. *Don't miss opportunities to monitor children's participation in fluency activities.* It is essential that you attend to what your students are doing as they participate in fluency activities. Students working with partners can get off task, engaging in conversations that have nothing to do with their reading. Similarly, students who should be echo or choral reading may not be participating at all. By walking around the room and clearly showing your students what your expectations are, you are likely to increase their participation and engagement and decrease the off-task behaviors that take away from learners' literacy experiences in the classroom.

8. *Don't spend too long on any one text—no matter how complex.* While we feel students should use challenging text, the text should not be so complex that you spend weeks—or even months—on it. We know of one teacher who had her class work on a single text for an entire year! While it is appropriate to provide students with the support necessary to deal with texts that they could not work with independently, any text that needs so much support that it overtakes your entire literacy curriculum for extended periods of time is likely to be too difficult for your learners.

---

university worked together to develop a weekly lesson plan that would help make the material more accessible for their students. The approach presented here, FORI (Stahl & Heubach, 2005), follows a basic format that allows for the *gradual release of responsibility* (Vygotsky, 1978) for reading a particular text over the course of the week. The lesson plan is based on a 5-day cycle, with the teacher providing full support for the material early on and lessening support as the week continues so that, by the week's end, the children should be able to carry out the reading on their own.

Introducing the Text (Day 1)

Because the FORI approach relies on repetition, a single text is selected for a 5-day lesson cycle. Following the weekly lesson plan (see Figure 2.1), the week begins with an introduction of a new text on Monday (assuming you

	Monday	Tuesday	Wednesday	Thursday	Friday
Fluency-Oriented Reading Instruction Basal lesson	Teacher introduces story. Teacher reads story to class; class discusses story. Option: Teacher develops graphic organizers. Option: Class does activities from basal.	Students practice story. Teacher and students echo-read story.	Students practice story. Teacher and students choral-read story.	Students practice story. Students partner-read story.	Students do extension activities. These may include writing in response to story, etc. Option: Teacher does running records of children reading.
Home reading	Children read 15–30 minutes in a book of their choosing.	Students take story home and practice reading basal story aloud to someone.	Students who need more practice take home the basal story; others take book of their choosing.	Students who need more practice take home the basal story; others take book of their choosing.	Children read 15–30 minutes in a book of their choosing.

FIGURE 2.1. Weekly FORI lesson plan.

are working with an uninterrupted school week). This introduction may include a range of preteaching activities such as building background knowledge, the use of webbing, or preteaching vocabulary. This component of the FORI program should include activities that you would typically use for a given selection (see Chapter 4 for more details). For example, if your story deals with life in the 1890s, you would want to build background knowledge by discussing how different your students' lives would have been without cars, television, or even radios!

After introducing the text, the next step involves reading the week's selection aloud to your class while your students follow along in their own copies. This step is important for a number of reasons. First, your reading provides students with a sense of the selection as a whole; by doing this, you are giving them an opportunity to understand the story before they have to read it themselves—a key principle in our programs. Second, your expressive, skilled rendering of the text serves as a model of fluent reading for your learners, allowing them to hear what their own reading should ultimately sound like. Finally, this reading presents your students with the opportunity to see the words as they are being pronounced, without the demands of trying to decode them independently.

Following the read-aloud, the students should participate in a discussion of the text. This discussion may involve traditional question-and-answer sequences but can encompass alternative approaches, such as graphic organizers (e.g., story maps) or response-oriented instruction. We consider a comprehension focus early in the lesson to be important because it emphasizes that the construction of meaning is the primary purpose for reading. Because young readers spend significant amounts of energy on word recognition, they may mistakenly develop the notion that correct word identification is the most important component of reading. By focusing students on the construction of meaning early in the lesson, you redirect students' attention toward comprehension—something they will hopefully build on in the future (Hoffman & Crone, 1985).

Echo Reading (Day 2)

On the second day (usually a Tuesday), instruction consists of an *echo reading* of the text. In this component, you read two or three sentences aloud to your students, who then "echo" what you have read by reading these same sentences back to you. The purpose of reading several sentences aloud at one time is to prevent your students from relying on their memory to repeat the text. Instead, they are forced to focus on the words in order to echo the passages correctly. You should also intersperse your echo reading of the text with questions to keep students focused on the text's meaning and prevent the procedure from becoming rote (see Chapter 4 for a more detailed lesson plan for echo reading; day 2 of the FORI approach and days

Echo reading consists of teachers reading a section of the text aloud and the students echoing that section back to the teacher as a group, tracking the text as they read it. It is important to start this process with a sentence or so. However, as students become more familiar with the technique and more competent with the material, it is important that the amount of text be extended into a paragraph or longer. This way, students are required to look at the words as they "echo" the selection back rather than just rely on their memory.

2, 4, and 5 of the Wide Reading approach). After completing the echo reading, you can give students activities associated with expanding their understanding of the text, such as written responses, or the opportunity to work on other aspects of the literacy curriculum.

Your students' at-home reading should also start on the second day so that they are sufficiently comfortable with the text to begin reading it on their own or with limited help. In order to achieve additional practice, you should ask your children to bring the text home and read it to either a family member or a friend. For the remainder of the week, their homework is determined by the amount of continued support they need to develop comfort with the selection. If a learner has achieved mastery of the text, he or she should have the opportunity to spend the time reading a book of his or her choosing. If, on the other hand, the child needs extra support, he or she should bring the week's selection home again to read for homework.

Choral Reading (Day 3)

The FORI lessons continue on day 3 (usually Wednesday) with you leading your students in a *choral reading* of the text. This activity is the shortest of the week because you and your class read the entire text in unison. It is important that you monitor the children during all the components of the instruction to ensure that they are actively engaged in the oral reading of the text. This monitoring can be achieved most easily by walking among the learners or by having the students who are most likely to be off-task sit near you or a more diligent student. As noted above, the students should either reread that week's selection or a book of their own choosing for homework on the third and fourth days as well.

Choral reading involves a simultaneous reading of the story by the teacher and the students. This approach provides students with support for word recognition and the use of expression, along with access to text they would not be able to read independently.

Partner Reading (Day 4)

The final rereading of the text involves a *partner reading* of the selection on day 4 (usually a Thursday). Partners can be selected in several ways (see Chapter 3 for suggestions), but we have found that self-selected partners and the pairing of more skilled readers with their less skilled peers highly effective in promoting both on-task behavior and cooperation between partners. Once the students are paired up, each is responsible for reading approximately a page of text (completing the sentence or paragraph they are currently working on, if it continues onto the next page), before allowing his or her partner to take over and read the next page. The partners act as coaches for one another, offering assistance and encouragement as needed. Upon completing their initial reading of the text, if time allows, students can switch pages and read through the selection a second time.

In partner reading, students choose or are assigned partners with whom they read or reread a text (depending upon the text's difficulty level). The students in the pair read the entire story or section of the story, taking turns by paragraphs or pages. As one partner reads, the other monitors the reading and helps when necessary. After the story is completed, a second reading can be initiated in which partners read opposite pages. (Ways to select partners and further discussion of this procedure can be found in Chapter 3.)

PHOTO 2.1. Partner reading (day 4).

Extension Activities (Day 5)

On the final day (usually a Friday), you can complete extension activities, such as written responses or further discussions of the text, with the children or, if the selection has been covered thoroughly, other literacy activities not associated with the text. Depending on the number of times students read the text at home, the total number of repetitions for each selection will range between four and seven readings over the course of the week. Although some discretion can be used regarding the number of days required to cover a given story or expository selection, depending on its length, we have found that the outlined lesson plan works extremely well for the vast majority of texts at these reading levels. In fact, we looked at a subset of 18 children, randomly selected from five classrooms, over the course of 1 week. On average, the students went from a reading rate of approximately 78 correct words per minute (cwpm) to nearly 120 cwpm, or, using Hasbrouck and Tindal's (1992) fluency norms, from the 25th to the 75th percentile. We consider this improvement to constitute significant progress indeed.

WIDE READING

The Wide Reading component incorporates the same principles presented in the FORI component; however, rather than reading a single text repeatedly over the course of a week, in this component, you and your students read three texts over the same 5-day period (see Figure 2.2).

Introducing the Text (Day 1)

The first day of the lesson plan (Monday, if you are able to work on an uninterrupted weekly schedule) parallels the FORI lesson. It starts with prereading activities for the primary text of the week, whether this involves building background knowledge, developing vocabulary, or making predictions. Next, you read the text aloud while your students follow along in their own copies. Finally, you and your students should discuss the selection. In addition, you could provide other opportunities to respond to the text, such as having the students complete a graphic organizer.

Echo Reading (Days 2, 4, and 5)

The second day (usually a Tuesday) also parallels the FORI program, with you and your students echo reading the story (see Chapter 4 for a more detailed lesson plan for the echo-reading component of the FORI and Wide Reading approach). Again, the procedure involves your reading a section of

	Monday	Tuesday	Wednesday	Thursday	Friday
Wide Reading Instruction	Teacher introduces story. Teacher reads story to class; class discusses story. Option: Teacher develops graphic organizers. Option: Class does activities from basal (story 1).	Students practice story. Teacher and students echo-read story 1. Option: Students do partner reading.	Students do extension activities. These may include writing in response to story, etc. Option: Teacher does running records of children reading.	Teacher and students echo or choral-read trade book (story 2). Option: Students partner-read story 2. Option: Students do extension activities (writing, etc.).	Teacher and students echo or choral-read trade book (story 3). Option: Students partner-read story 3. Option: Students do extension activities (writing, etc.).
Home reading	Children read 15–30 minutes per day in a book of their choosing.	Students take story home and practice reading basal story aloud to someone.	Children read 15–30 minutes per day in a book of their choosing.	Children read 15–30 minutes per day in a book of their choosing.	Children read 15–30 minutes per day in a book of their choosing.

FIGURE 2.2. Weekly Wide Reading lesson plan.

the text (usually several lines or a paragraph at a time) and having your students echo that text back to you. You also have the option, depending on the amount of time available, of allowing your students to partner-read the text after the completion of the echo reading. This provides the students with the opportunity to work with a partner in order to reread the entire selection.

Extension Activities (Day 3)

Where the Wide Reading approach begins to diverge from the FORI lesson plan is on the third day (usually a Wednesday). Rather than choral reading the material, you complete extension activities for the story with your students (this parallels day 5 of the FORI approach). These activities can include written responses, such as creating alternative endings or questions for discussion, or oral discussions that focus your students on plot or character development. Since the Wide Reading protocol addresses the week's primary selection in 3 days instead of 5, such activities are vital to strengthen the students' understanding of the text.

Echo Reading (Days 4 and 5)

The fourth and fifth days involve the echo reading and discussion of a second and third text with your students. Because the students are only working with the material for 1 day, it is important that you work with them to develop their understanding of the selection. Again, if time is available, you can ask the students to partner-read these texts after you have completed the echo reading and discussion of the text.

Although we understand it is not feasible for many districts to purchase two class sets of trade books for each week of the school year, we have found some ingenious ways of finding a second and third text for every week. First, it is often the case that numerous copies of a given book can be located in a school building, and it may be possible to pool resources to find enough texts for your class. For example, we worked with one school that had six copies of *Frog and Toad Are Friends* (Lobel, 1970) in each of four classrooms (plus a couple of copies in the library). Pooling these copies allowed each classroom to use the text while ensuring that every student had his or her own copy. Next, you can use alternatives to trade books to ensure that there are enough texts for each student to read from his or her own copy. For example, some schools have incorporated stories taken from sources such as *My Weekly Reader* or *Spider* magazine, or you could use older versions of basals or literature anthologies that your school still owns but that are no longer being used in the classroom. As with the FORI program, both the basal/literature anthology selection and the additional texts should be sent home for rereading by the students.

Thus, as you can see, although the Wide Reading program emphasizes the reading of multiple texts, a minor degree of repetition is incorporated in the approach.

WIDE READING OR FORI?

Why do we recommend the Wide Reading approach over the FORI? For two reasons. First, we found that the students in the Wide Reading group did somewhat better than their peers in the FORI group (although this difference was not significant—and both groups did better than their peers in the control classrooms). Second, research conducted by Mostow and Beck (2005) also indicates that students learned to read a new word more easily when they encountered it in different contexts than when they encountered it repeatedly in the same context, at least when the learners are provided with computer-based speech support. That is, students learn the word *blue* in the phrases "the *blue* car," "the *blue* dress," and "the *blue* sky" more readily than if they were to see the phrase "the *blue* car" three times. It may be that Wide Reading benefits children by indirectly providing repetition of words (and phrases) across a range of contexts.

Having said this, there is a plethora of evidence (e.g., Dowhower, 1989; Kuhn & Stahl, 2003) indicating that repetition can help learners more than simply reading a text once, at least in part because of the support provided. It may be that the ideal combination is the use of scaffolding with a range of texts, followed by the use of scaffolding with a single text read repeatedly.

PRINCIPLES FOR EFFECTIVE FLUENCY INSTRUCTION

Rasinski (2003) argues that four principles should underlie all good fluency instruction. The first is that children should be given a model of expressive reading. This principle may seem to emphasize an already common practice in the primary grades, but it is one that occurs less frequently in second and third grade than it does in kindergarten and first. Yet, it is worth highlighting for several reasons. First, reading aloud gives your students the opportunity to focus on the text's meaning as opposed to the words. When reading on their own, disfluent readers need to spend significant amounts of energy on their decoding, so little of their attention is available for constructing meaning. By giving them the chance to listen to a skilled reader, students are reinforced in their understanding that texts carry a message and that the ultimate reason for word identification is to determine that message. Further, by reading aloud to your students, you offer them an opportunity to engage with meaningful texts that they could not easily read

ORAL READING IN THE CURRICULUM: BEYOND ROUND ROBIN

Oral reading has had a varied role in the U.S. school curriculum (Rasinski & Hoffman, 2003). In past centuries, when the majority of jobs did not require high levels of literacy, formal schooling was often minimal. In addition, it was quite costly to produce reading materials, so they were not plentiful. As a result, individuals in the community who were skilled readers were often expected to read the texts that did exist, when needed, to their fellow citizens—either to share information (e.g., reading pamphlets to citizens during the Revolutionary War) or to entertain or enlighten (e.g., reading Bible tracts at home)—at least as often they were read silently. As a result, literacy instruction was often geared toward oral reading with an emphasis on individual interpretation of a given text. For example, if several students were assigned to read part of a classic, such as *Hamlet,* each student's use of prosodic elements could make for a highly personal interpretation of the piece (Hoffman & Crone, 1985).

Over the course of the 20th century, however, two factors shaped a major shift in literacy learning: In response to the needs of a changing economy, education became increasingly demanding and required of most workers, and, at the same time, texts, from novels to newspapers, became more readily available. As a result, most people in the United States became literate, and not only did they begin to read for themselves, they did so with their own purposes in mind. This shift was also reflected in the schools' literacy curricula, with silent reading replacing oral reading as the main form of instruction. Unfortunately, silent reading in the classroom comes with certain difficulties: When learners are reading silently, it is impossible to know whether they are making the expected progress or are even engaged with the text they are reading. To determine whether students were making progress or were on task, it was necessary to ask students to read aloud occasionally. Eventually, however, this process of randomly checking student progress came to be seen as useful, in and of itself, for a number of reasons (Ash & Kuhn, 2006). It was seen as a way (1) to ensure that every student spent some time reading, (2) to guarantee that the material was covered, (3) to help with specific aspects of reading development (fluency, word recognition, comprehension), and (4) to manage the classroom as well. As a result, the practice of *round robin reading* (and its present-day counterparts of popcorn, popsicle, and combat reading), wherein individual children take turns reading short segments of text aloud, was born.

Unfortunately, this practice quickly became the dominant instructional format for oral reading and the literacy curriculum, in general, in many schools—a practice that continues to exist in far too many classrooms today, despite the recognition by most reading professionals that it is an ineffective approach to literacy development (e.g., Optiz & Rasinski, 1998). In fact, it fails to meet student needs on all the points outlined above. For example, when individual students are asked to read a paragraph or two out of a selection, the round robin format does not provide them with enough practice to develop their reading skills. Next, although material may be "covered," round robin reading makes comprehension difficult by taking a unified text and breaking it into small parts that are hard to follow. Finally, it fails in terms of classroom management completely. Students who are skilled readers become bored when their less-skilled peers are reading, whereas the struggling readers often revert to off-task behaviors to avoid reading aloud entirely! Fortunately, a number of effective alternatives exist, including those discussed in this chapter, which can contribute to the reading development of your students (see, e.g., Rasinski, Blachowitcz, & Lems's [2006] *Fluency Instruction: Research-Based Best Practices*, for additional discussion of effective oral reading practices).

independently—potentially inspiring within them a desire to read on their own. Finally, by expressively reading aloud, you are providing students with an example of what their own reading should ultimately sound like.

Rasinski's second principle is that teachers should provide their students with support or assistance as they make the transition to fluent reading. Practices such as choral, echo, or paired reading provide this support and give children the chance to hear a smooth, expressive rendition of a text while they are reading it themselves. By scaffolding their reading in this manner, it is possible for learners to work with challenging material—material that they could not read on their own. This process also strengthens students' (1) word recognition by providing them with the pronunciation of the words they encounter, and (2) use of expression by helping them with appropriate phrasing. Such support guides your students through the reading of a particular text and helps them move beyond word-by-word reading by encouraging automatic, and *prosodic*, or expressive, reading.

The third principle is that practice is critical to fluency development. Providing your students with significant opportunities to practice reading connected text is central to developing their reading fluency (e.g., Samuels, 2004). Despite the recognition that students need ample opportunities to practice if they are going to become skilled readers (e.g., Allington, 1977; Gambrell, 1984), it is often the case that students spend far too much of their time engaged in activities that fail to help them become better readers, such as round robin reading (in any of its guises: popcorn, popsicle, or combat reading; e.g., Ash & Kuhn, 2006). Yet reviews of research on fluency instruction (Kuhn & Stahl, 2003; National Reading Panel, 2000) indicate that time spent practicing is critical if students are to *automatize* their knowledge of word recognition and apply what they are learning to their independent reading. By giving them opportunities to practice, you are helping your students become smooth and expressive readers.

The final principle emphasizes the importance of focusing on appropriate phrasing in fluency instruction. When your students read in a word-by-word manner, it reflects their lack of skill with decoding and their inability to apply their understanding of oral language to written text. As Rasinski (2003) states, meaning "lies in a text's phrases and not in its individual words" (p. 32). It should be noted that this phrasing is not always clear from the punctuation provided in the text. For example, pausing is not needed at many commas, and not every question mark requires a rise in pitch (for example, who, what, where, why questions). Therefore, it is important that you focus instruction on phrasing that replicates speech rather than on punctuation exclusively. Moreover, although speed is important, it is equally important not to turn fluency into an exercise in which your students' goal is to read with ever-increasing speed.

You can readily incorporate this fourth principle into your instruction by providing direct feedback on your students' use of expression, such as explaining how words should be grouped in a given sentence and by demonstrating how a story's meaning can be lost through inappropriate phrasing (e.g., read a story to your students in two-word phrases or in a word-by-word manner and ask them what it sounds like). As your students learn to use appropriate phrasing, their reading will sound more skilled and more expressive. And, by providing learners with reading instruction that integrates these four principles into the literacy curriculum, as we do with the FORI and Wide Reading programs, it is possible to help students make the transition from laborious word recognition and unexpressive renditions of text to reading that is "fluid, flowing and facile" (Dowhower, 1987, p. 390).

CLOSING THOUGHTS

Although we would recommend the Wide Reading approach over the FORI whenever it is possible to find sufficient materials, we consider both the FORI and Wide Reading approaches, with their scaffolding and simple classroom structure, to be useful methods for conducting shared reading instruction in second and third grades. Further, the teachers who have used these approaches have found them to be effective and easy to implement, and the students have genuinely enjoyed them. And, importantly in this period of high accountability, the research underlying them is scientifically based (Kuhn et al., 2006). As a result, we feel the results can be generalized and are comfortable recommending it across a range of socioeconomic levels and classroom settings. This research also indicates that fluency instruction, whether based upon repetition or the supported reading of a wider range of texts, is effective. It also has served to identify important elements for fluency instruction in general.

For us, the most critical feature is the amount of time our students spend reading connected text—a minimum of 20 minutes per day. In fact, when they did not spend significant amounts of time reading (e.g., only 5–12 minutes per day), children failed to make grade-appropriate gains in fluency. We cannot emphasize enough that both of these methods are designed to increase student engagement with print and that it is essential that your students read aloud at least 20–30 minutes per day during this very important phase in children's reading development. However, there is a second element to this equation. The engagement with text must be undertaken with extensive scaffolding because these methods employ texts that are challenging for most children. We feel that this procedure is especially important for *struggling readers* because it gives them the opportunity to work with grade-level text, even though much of this material is written at a level that is considerably higher than many of these learners can comfortably decode. Further, our research indicated that when the texts being used were not challenging enough, the students did not make significant progress. It is the scaffolding of challenging texts provided through the FORI and Wide Reading methods, whether through repetition or modeling (e.g., the use of echo, choral, and partner reading), that allows students to read text that would otherwise be considered frustrating.

This approach is quite different from the commonly used strategy of selecting a text based on children's reading level. Current best practice generally recommends that instructional level texts be read at approximately 95% level of accuracy, based on the Betts (1946) notion of instructional, independent, and frustration levels of learning. However, when the goal is fluency and the learners are provided with a variety of supports, such as are available with these fluency-oriented approaches, they are able to read texts at a higher difficulty level than would generally be suggested—texts that would normally be considered beyond their ability. Further, reading richer texts benefits children by exposing them to a wider variety and volume of words as well as a greater range of concepts. Both of these factors contribute to good decoding and comprehension skills (e.g., Beck, McKeown, & Kucan, 2002; Guthrie, 2004). They also serve to narrow the gap between more- and less-skilled readers that develops—and often widens—as students progress through their school years (Stanovich, 1986).

At the same time, we would not suggest that children should be given a text that is completely beyond them, even with support. Rather, we agree with Stahl and Heubach's (2005) suggestion that, with strong support, children can benefit from texts with which they have an accuracy rate of approximately 85%. Further, it is worth bearing in mind that the more difficult texts are for children's reading ability, the more support they will need from scaffolding, repetition, or additional reading at home. When the texts are closer to the children's reading level, it is likely that less scaffolding will be needed to support their reading development. In fact, scaffolding would likely be far less beneficial when students use text at their independent—or even the high end of their instructional—level, because they can handle such material with minimal support (e.g., Hollingsworth, 1970).

Despite the effectiveness of these approaches, fluency-oriented instruction is not for all children. For example, it is likely that children at an emergent reading level, or those unable to read preprimer texts independently, will not benefit from such instruction (e.g., Stahl & Heubach, 2005; see Chapter 5 for ideas on how to help these readers gain comfort with text). Typically, these are children for whom even the simplest texts are a struggle. Similarly, students who are already fluent readers are better off working with content-area text and challenging fiction, rather than engaging in the approaches outlined here. However, for many children to become successful readers, they need to make accelerated progress. Although this progress will look different across the grades and for different goals, one goal involves assisting children in developing their ability to read grade-level text with fluency and comprehension. Both the programs presented here can help students make such progress.

REFERENCES

Allington, R. L. (1977). If they don't read much, how they ever gonna get good? *Journal of Reading, 21,* 57–61.

Allington, R. L. (1983). Fluency: The neglected reading goal. *The Reading Teacher, 36,* 556–561.

Ash, G. E., & Kuhn, M. R. (2006). Meaningful oral and silent reading in the elementary and middle school classroom: Breaking the round robin reading addiction. In T. Rasinski, C. Blachowicz, & K. Lems (Eds.), *Fluency instruction: Research-based best practices* (pp. 155–172). New York: Guilford Press.

Beck, I. L., McKeown, M. G., & Kucan, L. (2002). *Bringing words to life: Robust vocabulary instruction.* New York: Guilford Press.

Betts, E. A. (1946). *Foundations of reading instruction.* New York: American Book.

Dowhower, S. L. (1987). Effects of repeated reading on second-grade transitional readers' fluency and comprehension. *Reading Research Quarterly, 22,* 389–406.

Dowhower, S. (1989). Repeated reading: Theory into practice. *The Reading Teacher, 42,* 502–507.

Fountas, I. C., & Pinnell, G. S. (1999). *Matching books to readers: Using leveled books in guided reading, K–3.* Portsmouth, NH: Heinemann.

Fountas, I. C., & Pinnell, G. S. (2005). *The Fountas and Pinnell leveled book list, K–8.* Portsmouth, NH: Heinemann.

Gambrell, L. B. (1984). How much time do children spend reading during teacher-directed reading instruction? In J. A. Niles & L. A. Harris (Eds.), *Changing perspectives on research in reading/language processing and instruction (33rd yearbook of the National Reading Conference,* pp. 193–198). Rochester, NY: National Reading Conference.

Gunning, T. G. (1998). *Best books for beginning readers.* Needham, MA: Allyn & Bacon.

Guthrie, J. (2004). *Teaching for literacy engagement: Practices, policies, and pitfalls.* Paper presented at the Governor's Literacy Forum, New Brunswick, NJ.

Hoffman, J. V., & Crone, S. (1985). The oral recitation lesson: A research-derived strategy for reading basal texts. In J. A. Niles & R. V. Lalik (Eds.), *Issues in literacy: A research perspective* (34th yearbook of the National Reading Conference, pp. 76–83). Rochester, NY: National Reading Conference.

Hollingsworth, P. M. (1970). An experiment with the impress method of teaching reading. *The Reading Teacher, 24*(2), 112–114.

Kuhn, M. R., Schwanenflugel, P. J., Morris, R. D., Morrow, L. M., Woo, D., et al. (2006). Teaching children to become fluent and automatic readers. *Journal of Literacy Research, 38,* 357–387.

Kuhn, M. R., & Stahl, S. A. (2003). Fluency: A review of developmental and remedial practices. *Journal of Educational Psychology, 95,* 3–22.

Loebel, A. (1970). *Frog and toads are friends.* New York: HarperCollins.

Mostow, J., & Beck, J. (2005, June). *Micro-analysis of fluency gains in a reading tutor that listens.* Paper presented at the annual meeting of the Society for the Scientific Study of Reading, Toronto, Ontario.

National Reading Panel. (2000). *Report of the subgroups: National Reading Panel.* Washington, DC: National Institute of Child Health and Development.

Optiz, M. F., & Rasinski, T. V. (1998). *Good-bye round robin reading: 25 effective oral reading strategies.* Portsmouth, NH: Heinemann.

Pikulski, J. J., & Chard, D. J. (2005). Fluency: Bridge between decoding and reading comprehension. *The Reading Teacher, 58,* 510–519.

Rasinksi, T. V. (2003). *The fluent reader: Oral reading strategies for building word recognition, fluency, and comprehension.* New York: Scholastic Professional Books.

Rasinski, T. V., & Hoffman, J. V. (2003). Oral reading in the school curriculum. *Reading Research Quarterly, 38,* 510–522.

Samuels, S. J. (2004). Toward a theory of automatic information processing in reading, revisited. In R. B. Ruddell & N. J. Unrau (Eds.), *Theoretical models and processes of reading* (5th ed., pp. 1127–1148). Newark, DE: International Reading Association.

Stahl, S. A., & Heubach, K. M. (2005). Fluency-oriented reading instruction. *Journal of Literacy Research, 37,* 25–60.

Stanovich, K. E. (1986). Matthew effects in reading: Some consequences of individual differences in the acquisition of literacy. *Reading Research Quarterly, 21,* 360–407.

Vygotsky, L. (1978). *Mind in society.* Cambridge, MA: Harvard University Press.

CHAPTER 3

Classroom Practices for Supporting Fluency Development

ELIZABETH B. MEISINGER and BARBARA A. BRADLEY

THIS CHAPTER INCLUDES:

- A description of echo reading, choral reading, and partner reading strategies.
- A discussion of the research on the effectiveness of echo reading, choral reading, and partner reading.
- An outline of how to successfully organize, implement, and manage echo reading, choral reading, and partner reading in the classroom.
- An exploration of other ways to use or structure echo reading, choral reading, and partner reading.

As mentioned throughout the book, in order for your students to become fluent readers, they need to spend a significant amount of time practicing their reading skills, because this practice provides them with the opportunity to develop their *automaticity* and *prosody*. However, many children spend 7 minutes or less a day reading connected text at school (Gambrell, 1984; Kuhn, Schwanenflugel, Morrow, & Bradley, 2006); clearly not enough time to develop the levels of skilled reading that are necessary to become a successful, independent reader. One of the most important aspects of the Wide Reading and Fluency-Oriented Reading Instruction (FORI) approaches is their integration of significantly greater amounts of time reading *connected text* into your curriculum (between 20 and 45 minutes, depending on the day). In this chapter, we describe three pedagogical strategies that increase the amount of time your students read connected text: echo reading, choral reading, and partner reading. We hope that this chapter will help you feel comfortable implementing these strategies in your classroom or, if you already use these strategies, discover ways to improve their implementation.

ECHO READING

What Is Echo Reading?

Echo reading is a teacher-assisted oral reading strategy in which you read a section of a text aloud as your children silently follow along in their own copy of the text. Upon completing a section, your children read the same section aloud in unison. This strategy provides a considerable amount of reading support to your children because you model accurate word reading, pacing, inflection, and tone of voice. Perhaps most importantly, you also control the amount of text read at one time, based upon its difficulty, thus making the text accessible to your children. Echo reading is an important component of both the FORI and Wide Reading programs (see Chapter 2). In the FORI program, echo reading is used as part of the *scaffolded repeated reading* in which a teacher provides a considerable amount of reading support to children. Echo reading is introduced on day 2, after children have already experienced preteaching activities and a teacher read-aloud of the text on day 1. Echo reading is also used on day 2 of the Wide Reading program as a means of ensuring that students are comfortable with the week's primary text. However, it also is used to support your students' reading of their second and third

---

WHAT DOES RESEARCH SAY ABOUT THE EFFECTIVENESS OF ECHO READING?

Although there is no research studying the effectiveness of echo reading as a single strategy for promoting fluency, echo reading has been found to promote the development of vocabulary and comprehension of elementary-age students (Schneeberg, 1977). It also has been included in several studies of effective oral reading interventions (Hoffman, 1987; Homan, Klesius, & Hite, 1993; Morris & Nelson, 1992; Stahl et al., 1997). For example, in a study comparing echo and choral reading to repeated reading, echo and choral reading were found to be as effective as repeated reading for promoting fluency and comprehension (Homan et al., 1993). James Hoffman (1987) also included echo reading in an intervention to support struggling second-grade readers (Hoffman, 1987). Although he found "no miracles" (p. 372), these previously unsuccessful readers made progress in their reading. Further, the students shifted their focus from accurate word identification to fluency and comprehension.

text on days 4 and 5. Because the second and third texts are only taught for a day, it is essential that comprehension activities be integrated into these lessons as well (see Chapter 4 for suggestions).

How Should I Carry Out Echo Reading in My Classroom?

Because echo reading is a strategy that provides your children with considerable reading support, we suggest that it be implemented shortly after a new text is introduced. Whether you are using echo reading as part of the FORI or Wide Reading or as part of your traditional classroom activities, we recommend that echo reading be implemented in the following manner (Stahl & Heubach, 2005).

- *Provide each child with his or her own copy of the text to be read.* Tell your children to open their books to the correct page number and to find the first word of the first section to be read. Because children will be following along silently while you read aloud, as well as later echo reading aloud, they need their own text in order to follow along and finger-point read.
- *Explain the echo reading procedures to the children.* Explain to your children:

> "We will be echo reading the text we read yesterday [or we will be echo reading a new text today]. I will read a section out loud. As I read aloud, I want you to read along silently. After I finish reading a section aloud, you will read it back to me out loud. Are there any questions?"

It is important that you walk around the class making sure that all the children are on the correct page and pointing to the first word to be read.

- *Practice the echo reading procedures before reading the entire text.* Until children have learned the procedures, have them practice echo-reading a few sentences from the text before attempting to read the entire text with them. When introducing echo reading, it is important that you only read a sentence or so aloud until children become familiar with this strategy. Explain to the children:

> "We are going to practice by echo reading a few sentences before we read the entire text. I will read a sentence aloud and you should read silently with me. [Scan the class to see that each child is ready to read.] Is everyone ready? Let's begin. [Read a sentence aloud.] Now it's your turn to read with me. Make sure your eyes are on the text. Are you ready?"

Read the sentence aloud with your children. Continue this process until they understand that they are to echo back the text you have read to them.

Once your children understand the echo reading procedures, it will only be necessary for you to read aloud with the children when they are struggling with the text, reading at a slow pace, or reading with poor expression. However, always be sure that children are at the correct place before echo reading a text. A quick walk around the room will affirm that.

• *Monitor the children's reading.* As you are echo reading with them, walk around the class to monitor whether children are reading and enunciating the words appropriately. Because the texts should be at the students' grade level or above, this task may be somewhat challenging for children reading below grade level. Therefore, it may be necessary to stand near these children and provide additional support as they echo-read aloud. For example, you may occasionally need to stop at a child's desk and point to the words in his or her text as you, or he or she, reads aloud.

• *Facilitate comprehension of the text.* Comprehension is the primary purpose of reading. Therefore, even when you are focusing on decoding and fluency, it is important to stop and discuss difficult vocabulary and to clarify text that may be confusing for your children. Always emphasize comprehension with your students. Guidance on how to provide comprehension support during fluency instruction can be found in Chapter 4.

Echo reading is a strategy designed to support children when they are first introduced to a new text or when they are reading a particularly challenging text. For echo reading to be successful, the entire class should be engaged in the activity. However, as you know, some children may stray off task easily when they are supposed to be echo reading aloud with the class. Also, some students may mumble words or sounds when they are reading aloud with other children. Therefore, it is important to "set the tone" when engaging your children in this whole-class activity. This can be done by reading clearly, walking around the room, and using positive comments ("I like how well you read this section!") to redirect students when needed, and interspersing questions throughout the reading to refocus their attention on the meaning of the text. Further, be sure that all your children have thoroughly learned the echo reading procedures and that they understand that they are not simply "listening" while you read about but are reading silently with you. Following these guidelines will help you to successful implement this strategy with your class.

CHORAL READING

What Is Choral Reading?

Choral reading is another teacher-assisted oral reading strategy in which the teacher and children simultaneously read a section of a text aloud. However, choral reading provides children with a moderate amount of

WHAT DOES RESEARCH SAY ABOUT THE EFFECTIVENESS OF CHORAL (UNISON) READING?

Research indicates that choral reading, sometimes referred to as *unison reading*, is an effective strategy for facilitating children's reading achievement and may be presented in many variations (e.g., reading with an adult, reading along with taped book; Cox & Shrigley, 1980; Dowhower, 1987; Gamby, 1987). In one study, choral reading was found to increase the reading accuracy of elementary school students (Cox & Shrigley, 1980). In another study, reading skills—such as the ability to sound out words, fluency, and comprehension—in elementary school students with developmental delays were supported by repeated choral readings of predictable text (Mefford & Pettegrew, 1997). Choral reading also has been included in a teacher-assisted nonrepetitive reading program in which students demonstrated growth in both fluency and comprehension (Homan et al., 1993).

reading support compared to echo reading. This is because rather than reading the text to the students, then having them read it aloud, the teacher and students read it together. The teacher sets the pace of the reading, provides supported word recognition, and models proper inflection and tone of voice that the children may imitate while reading aloud.

Choral reading is an important component of the FORI program and is introduced on day 3, after children have already experienced preteaching activities, a teacher read-aloud (day 1), and an echo reading of the text (day 2). This rereading is designed as a transition between the more fully scaffolded echo reading and the partner reading that occurs the next day, in which the student is responsible for reading half of the text. In the Wide Reading program, on the other hand, choral reading, although an option, is less integral to the program. It is used as a means of supplementing the lessons, depending on available time. For example, if your students have completed their echo reading of a text and you wish to do a second reading but do not feel there is enough time for another echo reading or a partner reading, you may choose to choral-read the text. It is often the case that a choral reading can be integrated into another lesson, allowing your students the option of another supported reading of the material.

How Should I Carry Out Choral Reading in My Classroom?

Choral reading, like echo reading, has simple procedures that your children must learn in order to engage in this activity successfully. Once the procedures are learned, there are several variations of this strategy that you may use to increase their engagement. Based on previous FORI research (Stahl

& Heubach, 2005), we recommend that choral reading be implemented in the following manner.

- *Provide children with their own copy of the text.* As with echo reading, your children need their own copy of the text, and they need to be able to locate the first word of the first paragraph to be read on the specified page.
- *Explain the choral reading procedures to the children.* Explain to your children:

> "Today, we will be choral reading the text we read yesterday [or earlier today]. Choral reading is when we read the text out loud as a group. As I read, and you read aloud with me, I want you to try to imitate the way I read the sentences. Make sure you pause at the end of the sentences and put some life into your voice! Also, remember to read loud enough so that your voice can be heard, but not too loud so it sounds as if you were screaming!"

Before beginning, answer any questions your children may have about the reading.

- *Practice the choral reading procedures before reading the entire text.* Before reading the entire text, you should practice choral reading a few sentences or paragraphs to help your children learn the procedures. Explain to your children:

> "Before we begin, we are going to practice. Read along with me."

Make sure that all students are reading the sentences or paragraphs you have selected during the choral reading. If you notice some children not reading along or mumbling words, provide extra support by standing next to them when reading or by pointing to the words as they are read. Practice reading with the children until the passage sounds clear and generally fluent, and it appears that all the students are reading along with you.

When initially introducing choral reading to your children, it may be necessary for you to read at a slightly slower pace than you would typical use when reading aloud. Also, be sure to enunciate each word and read expressively, but do not read it in an overly dramatic fashion. Once children understand the choral reading process and the purpose of punctuation and text features (e.g., emphasize words written in all capitalized letters), then it will be possible to read with even more expression.

- *Monitor the children's reading and facilitate their comprehension of the text.* As with echo reading, you should walk around the class to monitor whether your children are reading and enunciating the words appropriately and provide additional support as needed. Also, you can stop to discuss difficult vocabulary or sections in the text that may continue to be confusing.

We have also found that introducing variation helps to increase children's engagement in choral reading. Once the students become familiar with the choral reading process, you may want to try these variations as well:

- Have the girls read one section together and then the boys read the next section.
- Divide the class in half. Have children sitting on the left side of the room read a section together, followed by the children sitting on the right side of the room.
- Have children whose last names begin with A–L read a section, followed by children whose last names begin with M–Z.
- If a story has a lot of dialogue, individual children can volunteer to read it while the rest of the class reads the narration together (this procedure differs from round robin reading because the students will have had opportunities to practice the text in a supported manner before attempting to read a passage on their own).
- Finally, encourage children to put life into their voices as they read. Ask them to emphasize scary parts of a story by reading in a low voice. Or if there are widely differing characters, say a mouse and a bear, why not read sentences said by the mouse in a high-pitched voice and those said by the bear in a low deep voice?
- Basically, mix it up! Have fun. Remember, the way you read sets the tone, and you can project enthusiasm about reading aloud. Further, reading and experiencing the text in these different ways may help children to remember important parts of the story.

PARTNER READING

Partner reading is another fun and effective pedagogical strategy for promoting the development of reading fluency. Like echo and choral reading, it is designed to increase the amount of time children spend reading aloud in the classroom while providing the support many struggling readers need to successfully negotiate text. However, it is a procedure that is best initiated after children have developed some familiarity with the text through procedures discussed elsewhere in this and other chapters. As such, it is a natural strategy to use following an echo or choral reading of the book. In FORI, partner reading occurs on the fourth day (although it may be introduced on day 3, depending on the length of the text and the time available). In the Wide Reading approach, partner reading can be used to supplement

PAIRED OR PARTNER READING?

Partner reading is a form of *paired reading*, a tutoring strategy originally developed by Morgan (1976) for use by parents, but it has also been used for peer- and teacher-implemented tutoring (e.g., Topping & Lindsay, 1992). Paired reading generally involves the pairing of a more capable reader (e.g., parent, teacher, or peer) with a less capable one. In contrast to partner reading, the readers do not take turns. Rather, the tutor reads simultaneously with the less capable reader. If the child feels that he or she can read independently, then the child signals the tutor and reads independently until an unknown word is encountered, at which point simultaneous reading resumes. Whereas the aim of paired reading is to provide needed assistance and practice to the tutee, partner reading is a classroom strategy whose aim is to provide supported practice in the reading of connected text for all children by including a turn-taking procedure.

the echo reading that is done several times a week, depending on the time available.

What Is Partner Reading?

In partner reading, children are paired to provide one another with support in the oral reading of connected text (Meisinger, Schwanenflugel, Bradley, & Stahl, 2004; Stahl, Heubach, & Crammond, 1997). In this strategy, one child reads aloud while his or her partner listens, follows along, and provides support and assistance. This support can take a number of forms:

- Partners may help sound out words (e.g., "*Th*" sounds like this, "*thhhhh*"), provide the reader with unknown words (e.g., "That word is *trouble*, it's a weird word"), and correct misread words; e.g., "Oops, that word was *that*, not *than*").
- Children may also remind their partners how to implement general strategies for decoding words in the context of reading aloud, such as those described in Chapter 5 (e.g., asking "Does this rhyme with a word you already know?" or asking their partners to sound out the word and then check it against the meaning of the sentence to see if it makes sense).
- Children may provide encouragement and emotional support for their partners, something that is especially important for struggling readers (e.g., "Keep at it. You're getting there! That was great!").
- Alternatively, children may do something as simple as helping their partners find their place on the page.

Each of these types of support should be modeled for your students to help them develop comfort with the procedure.

In the partner reading strategy, children alternate the roles of the reader and the supporter every other page as they read a book or story together. In this way, children get small breaks from their oral reading while they provide one another with assistance for unknown words or other difficulties encountered in the text. In order to give each child a chance to read the whole story, children can complete a second reading with their partners, this time reading opposite pages to those they read initially. As with echo and choral reading, each child should read from his or her own copy of the book (whether the book is part of the basal series, literature analogies, or trade books or magazines such as *My Weekly Reader*).

Partner reading is an important component of both the FORI and Wide Reading programs. In the FORI program, partner reading is used as part of the scaffolded repeated reading that comprises the program; with this strategy the children practice reading the same text throughout the week with gradually less support as they develop mastery of the text. Because partner reading involves the least amount of support, it is not usually introduced until day 4, after children have already experienced the text in several guises, including preteaching activities and a read-aloud (day 1), a choral reading (day 2), and an echo reading of the text (day 3). As students become more familiar with the procedure, you may want them to partner-read the text on day 3 as well, depending on the time available and your daily schedule. In contrast, partner reading in the Wide Reading program is used to gain supported practice in the reading of a variety of texts over the course of a given week. The frequency of partner reading in the Wide Reading program is dependent on the length of a given text and the amount of time available. As a result, teachers have the *option* of asking

PHOTO 3.1. Two children partner reading.

WHAT DOES RESEARCH SAY ABOUT THE EFFECTIVENESS OF PARTNER READING?

Research has indicated that partner reading can be an important component of successful reading programs. For example, several comprehensive literacy programs for elementary school children that embrace a cooperative learning framework, such as Cooperative Integrated Reading and Composition (CIRC; Madden, Stevens, & Slavin, 1986) and Success for All (Slavin & Madden, 2000), include partner reading. It is also a central component of several effective literacy programs, such as FORI (Stahl & Heubach, 2005), Wide Reading (see Chapter 2), and Peer-Assisted Learning Strategies (PALS; Fuchs, Fuchs, Mathes, & Simmons, 1997), whose aim is to facilitate the development of fluent reading skills. Some variation in the implementation of partner reading exists across these programs. For example, in CIRC and Success for All, both children in the pair read the material silently before taking turns reading aloud from the text. In PALS, the more-skilled readers read the story for 5 minutes; this is followed by 5 minutes of reading from the less-skilled reader along with a retelling of the story by the less-skilled reader. However, all of the approaches share the same essential components: two children take turns reading along in a given text and provide one another assistance. Although partner reading is only one component of these literacy programs, their inclusion indicates that it can be incorporated easily in an overall literacy curriculum.

Partner reading is effective. In one study carried out in third-grade classrooms (Vaughn et al., 2000), the children who partner-read two to three times per week for 12 weeks showed an average 29% increase in reading rate on a standardized test of oral reading fluency, although their comprehension and reading accuracy were not affected in a positive manner. Further, in the Classwide Peer Tutoring (CWPT; Simmons, Fuchs, Fuchs, Hodge, & Mathes, 1994) program, in which high- and low-skilled readers were paired for the purpose of taking turns reading aloud to one another, participating students read a significantly greater number of words correctly (Simmons et al., 1994) than did their peers who did not participate. Further, when studied longitudinally, the participating students demonstrated greater gains in their overall reading skill, as well as increases in their oral reading rates, when compared to control students (Greenwood, Delquadri, & Hall, 1989).

Research suggests that partner reading is effective for several reasons. First, children benefit from practicing the reading of connected text (National Reading Panel, 2000), and this approach ensures that students spend significant amounts of time reading aloud or following along with their partner. Second, partner reading provides learners with the opportunity to read a text repeatedly, which supports the development of automatic word reading (Samuels, 2004). Third, because children receive correction and support from their partner during the reading, they are able to practice a text that they cannot yet read independently (Rasinski, 2003). Taken together, these factors promote accelerated progress in the development of reading fluency.

the students to partner-read a given text as a follow-up to the echo reading component of the program (days 2, 3, 4 and 5), but, unlike FORI, there is no definite pattern to its use in the Wide Reading program.

How Should I Carry Out Partner Reading in My Classroom?

When children work cooperatively for the purpose of accomplishing a shared goal, academic productivity and achievement are enhanced. From our research we have identified several ways that you can promote cooperative interactions and on-task behavior from your students during partner reading. Following are several recommendations on how you can organize, implement, and manage partner reading in classrooms (Meisinger et al., 2004):

• *Provide adequate instruction of the basic partner reading script.* Begin by explaining partner reading to your students. Tell your students:

> "Today you are going to read a story with a partner. When you partner-read, you take turns reading pages. During partner reading each partner has a job. One partner reads the page [or paragraph] out loud and with expression. When one of you is reading aloud, it is the other's job to read the words silently with him or her to make sure he or she is saying all the words right. If your partner gets stuck on a word, you should help him or her out if you can do that in a helpful way. When you finish the page, switch roles with your partner and you read the next page. Your partner then helps you. When you are finished with the story, you may have time to read the story again but swap pages. Pages that you read before will now be read by your partner. Pages that your partner read will now be read by you."

• *Practice what it means to be a good partner.* Go over the jobs of each partner with your class and discuss what being a good partner involves and post a summary of the following points (see Figure 3.1). Good partners listen to each other and read along silently when it is not their turn to read aloud. Good partners help each other read misread words. They provide unknown words, or even better, help each other remember to use word-reading strategies learned in class. Good partners do not laugh or jeer at each other's misread or unknown words, but simply provide the words. Good partners help each other find their place, if needed, and encourage each other to go on when tired or frustrated. Good partners also raise their hand to get their teacher's attention if a problem arises during partner reading, such as an argument between the two partners or when neither of the partners is able to decipher a difficult word. Good partners have a positive attitude and stay on task during partner reading.

How to Be a Good Partner

- Have a positive attitude.
- Provide unknown words appropriately.
- Correct misread words in a positive manner.
- Listen continuously and keep your eyes on the story.
- Give your best reading effort and read with expression.
- Alert teacher to problems.
- No off-subject talking.

FIGURE 3.1. The good partner posting.

Review examples of positive support (e.g., "The word is *captain*, "We are on page 12." "We are almost done") versus negative statements (e.g., "You're stupid if you don't know that word"). Review examples of what off-task behavior looks like. For example, in partner reading, talking about something unrelated to the story, looking around the room instead of listening and following along as the partner reads, or not reading aloud when it's one's turn would be off-task behavior.

- *Practice and model partner reading behaviors.* Partner reading is most successful when your children understand exactly what behaviors they should exhibit during this activity. To manage noise, you should emphasize the "6-inch-voice rule." To explain this rule, show your students a 12-inch ruler. Explain the difference between a 12-inch voice (by speaking loudly) and a 6-inch voice (using a softer voice). Have your students use 12-inch and 6-inch voices with their neighbors. After illustrating the rule, explain that while partner reading, they must use a 6-inch voice." Another behavior you should explain and request is the "shoulder-to-shoulder rule." Explain to your students that when they partner read, they must be shoulder to shoulder if they are going to be able to hear their partner and not have to talk loud. Illustrate by having two students talk in front of the class as they stand about 2 feet apart. After this, have the students talk shoulder to shoulder.

Now, choose one of your students to come to the front of the room to partner-read with you. Model with the student for the class what partner reading looks like, using the 6-inch-voice rule and reading shoulder to shoulder. It is also important to model good partner reading behavior, such as providing helpful assistance when a word is unknown, correcting mis-read words in a positive manner, raising your hand when a problem is encountered, keeping your eyes on the page and listening attentively to your partner when he or she is reading, and reading with expression.

Further, your children should be instructed on what they are to read, for how long, and where they will read. Typically students are allowed to partner-read at their desks, on the floor, in comfortable nooks and crannies around the room (e.g., bean bags, reading corner, rocking chairs), and sometimes even under desks. As long as children are in your view, the specific location is not important. You should also set guidelines for any off-limit areas, and this component should go smoothly also (e.g., no reading in the hallway).

• *Allow children to choose their own partners.* Children know with whom they get along and generally choose a partner with whom they will interact cooperatively (Meisinger et al., 2004). You may want to instruct students to choose their partner by groups or by sections to ease the process (e.g., "The students at table 1 may now choose their partners"). However, if one of your children demonstrates poor judgment when choosing a partner, it may be necessary to intervene and assign a new partner. Alternatively, if you assign partners, seating arrangement (pairing children who sit next to one another) or reading ability (pairing higher-ability readers with lower-ability readers) are commonly used categories.

Although it is recommended that children choose their own partners, *high–high and low–low ability pairings should be avoided.* For children to carry out of the roles of both the *reader* and *supporter*, it is essential that a *need for assistance* and an *ability to provide assistance* are present within the pair. When this requirement is not met, more off-task behavior is observed (Meisinger et al., 2004). This means that if two of your struggling readers choose one another as partners, neither may be able to provide the assistance that the other needs with unknown words, potentially causing a breakdown in the partner reading interaction. Conversely, if two very good readers are paired together, neither child requires assistance, and the children may become disengaged from the task. If your students self-select low–low or high–high ability pairings, it may be useful to determine partners for your class using the method described above. If you are not following the FORI or Wide Reading approaches, it is important that you choose challenging, substantial texts (within reason), such as are found in the grade-level anthology.

One easy way to accomplish the partnering of children based on reading level is to create a two-column list in which you place your most-skilled reader on the top of the first column and the student who is experiencing the most difficulty with his or her reading on the bottom of the second column (see Figure 3.2). Below the most-skilled reader, list your next most-skilled reader in the first column. Similarly, list the student who is second in terms of reading difficulties above the student who is most struggling. Continue with this process until you have filled in the names of the middle students in your class (either in the bottom spots of the first column or the top spots in the second column). You should then match your students across the columns to create pairs. By matching students in this manner, you ensure a difference in reading level between the learners, but not so great a difference that either the skilled reader or struggling reader will become frustrated with his or her partner (Strickland, Ganske, & Monroe, 2002).

To prevent struggles over who should read first, teachers sometimes assign a particular child to begin reading the first page, although this is not usually necessary once children are comfortable with the partner reading process. If you decide to assign your students, you can designate one child within each pair as partner "A" and the other as partner "B." Partner "A" will read the first page (or paragraph), and partner "B" will read the second, and so on, and, when the story is reread, partner "B" will read the first page (or paragraph), and partner "A" will read the second one.

In the FORI and Wide Reading approaches, your children will be reading from grade-level texts or higher (e.g., if most of your students are already reading at grade level, an above-grade-level text should be used). If you are not using a basal reader or literature anthology for your text, you

Skill rank	Child	Skill rank	Child
1	Shanique	11	Randall
2	Salvador	12	Lakeisha
3	Jason	13	Chloe
4	Quantavious	14	Leo
5	Emily	15	Steve
6	DeJuan	16	Angel
7	Paul	17	Willy
8	Sophie	18	Dan
9	Desiree	19	Gabriel
10	Luis	20	Carolina

FIGURE 3.2. An example of how to pair more-skilled readers with less-skilled readers.

should choose texts that are at least the length of a typical basal reader story. Although partner reading can be used for shorter texts such as poems, it is geared toward texts that allow children to take turns engaging in sustained reading. Texts that are very short will not provide enough opportunity for practice. In fact, it is possible that you will spend more time just getting children into position than they will spend reading if you use shorter texts.

Once your children understand what partner reading is and what they need to do to be a good partner, have them get their books out and turn to the selected page. Tell your students:

> "It is time to begin partner reading. Remember to use your 6-inch voices and follow along with your partner to check his or her reading. If you finish reading before time is up, switch places and read the story over again with your partner. When I call your table, you may choose your partner [or I will assign you each a partner], find a place to read, and begin."

• *Teachers need to monitor partner reading.* Once the partner reading routine has been established, your children will generally require little prompting or redirection, because it is a simple and enjoyable activity. However, while the children partner-read, you should walk around the room listening to them read, helping pairs that are stuck on an unknown word, redirecting those who are off task, or modeling expressive reading when needed. Partner reading provides a wonderful opportunity for you to listen to your children read and allows you to monitor their progress throughout the year.

Teachers involved in the FORI and Wide Reading instruction have sometimes expressed the concern that their class may get out of control during partner reading. In our experience, this concern is generally unwarranted. Because each child has a specific task during the activity, little off-task behavior is typically observed once all students have learned the roles that compose partner reading. Indeed, the more instruction provided to students at the beginning of the year about the partner-reading process, the less teachers tend to monitor for behavioral issues later in the year (Meisinger et al., 2004) (see Figure 3.3).

Other Applications of Partner Reading

You can utilize partner reading in several other ways. As indicated in Chapter 7, partner reading is a great strategy to share with parents and caregivers. It is a simple, structured, and fun way for caregivers to read and spend time with their children. It can be taught in just a few minutes on back-to-school night, or it can even be explained in a flyer sent home. For

Partner Reading Checklist

✓ Teach the partner reading process.
- Explain the role of the reader.
- Explain the role of the supporter.
- Explain the "6-inch-voice" rule.
- Explain the "should-to-shoulder" rule.
- Explain that students switch roles every other page.
- When done, students should reread the story so that each partner reads the opposite pages or has read all of the pages.
- Students should raise their hand for the teacher if a problem is encountered.

✓ Model partner reading for the children.

✓ Decide where children can read (e.g., at their desks, on the floor, under desks, in reading stations). What locations are off limits?

✓ Decide which text will they read and for how long.

✓ Decide how you will select partners.
- Children choose their own partners.
  or
- Teacher assigns partners.

✓ Watch for low–low and high–high ability pairings.
- Adjust difficulty level of the text or assign new partners.

✓ Monitor partner reading.
- Assist pairs with difficult words.
- Listen to students' oral reading.
- Redirect any off-task behavior.
- Monitor reading progress throughout the year.

FIGURE 3.3. Checklist that teachers may follow in carrying out partner reading in their classrooms.

example, children could model partner reading for their caregivers on conference night or during school open houses. Caregivers may not always know effective approaches for reading with their children, and partner reading provides a simple structure for reading at home while establishing a positive interaction with their children around text. Also, because the child and his or her caregiver *take turns* reading, struggling readers may be more amenable to partner reading as opposed to reading an entire text aloud each night. Further, children can then partner-read with additional members of their family (e.g., grandparents, brothers, sisters). The more time children spend practicing their reading skills, the better they develop these skills.

In fact, because of its structured yet social nature, partner reading has been used successfully as part of an intervention aimed at reducing and preventing behavioral problems in school (Boyle et al., 1999). Thus, this strategy may promote positive behavior in learners while simultaneously facilitating the development of fluent reading skills.

In the classroom, it is also possible for you to supplement partner reading with comprehension activities. For example, after completing their partner reading, your children could retell what they read to their partner. Partners could also work together to summarize the story orally or in written form.

Partner reading can also be used as a tutoring strategy (Topping & Lindsay, 1992). In order to use partner reading in this manner, a struggling reader is paired with a more fluent reader (e.g., teacher, volunteer, another student) to gain additional reading practice. For example, a struggling second grader could be paired with a fluent fourth grader to partner-read several times a week. Or a struggling second grader could read an easier text with a first grader or kindergartner. The fact that the struggling reader would have the opportunity to be the more knowledgeable of the pair could give him or her the confidence to want to succeed!

CLOSING THOUGHTS

Research suggests that echo reading, choral reading, and partner reading are effective strategies for promoting the development of fluent oral reading skills. We have had success with these strategies as part of the FORI and Wide Reading approaches. In addition to being enjoyable pedagogical strategies, they are relatively easy to organize, implement, and manage. They can be used with the whole classroom (as they are in FORI and Wide Reading), in small groups, or as a tutoring strategy with parents, teachers, and students. You may also wish to supplement these oral reading strategies with comprehension activities, as was discussed above and in the next chapter. We think that these strategies will foster student engagement with connected text and is well worth the class time spent on them.

REFERENCES

Boyle, M. H., Cunningham, C. E., Heale, J., Hundert, J., McDonald, J., Offord, D. R., et al. (1999). A tri-ministry study: Evaluation methodology. *Journal of Child Psychology and Psychiatry and Allied Disciplines, 40,* 1051–1060.

Cox, R. M., & Shrigley, R. L. (1980). Comparing three methods of practicing reading to reduce errors in oral reading. *Reading Improvement, 17*(4), 306–310.

Dowhower, S. L. (1987). Effects of repeated reading on second-grade transitional readers' fluency and comprehension. *Reading Research Quarterly, 22*(4), 389–406.

Fuchs, D., Fuchs, L. S., Mathes, R. G., & Simmons, D. C. (1997). Peer-assisted learning strategies: Making classrooms more responsive to diversity. *American Educational Research Journal, 34,* 174–206.

Gambrell, L. B. (1984). How much time do children spend reading during teacher-directed reading instruction? In J. A. Niles & L. A. Harris (Eds.), *Changing perspectives on research in reading/language processing and instruction: 33rd yearbook of the National Reading Conference* (pp. 193–198). Rochester, NY: National Reading Conference.

Gamby, G. (1987). Talking books and taped books. *The Reading Teacher, 36,* 366–369.

Greenwood, C. R., Delquadri, J. C., & Hall, R. V. (1989). Longitudinal effects of classwide peer tutoring. *Journal of Educational Psychology, 81,* 371–383.

Hoffman, J. V. (1987). Rethinking the role of oral reading in basal instruction. *Elementary School Journal, 87*(3), 367–373.

Homan, S. P., Klesius, J. P., & Hite, C. (1993). Effects of repeated readings and nonrepetitive strategies on students' fluency and comprehension. *Journal of Educational Research, 87*(2), 94–99.

Kuhn, M. R., Schwanenflugel, P. J., Morrow, L. M., & Bradley, B. (2006, May). *The development of fluent and automatic reading: scaling up—year 2.* Poster presented at the International Reading Association annual meeting, Chicago.

Madden, N. A., Stevens, R. J., & Slavin, R. E. (1986). *Reading in the mainstream: A cooperative learning approach* (Tech. Rep. No 5). Baltimore: Center for Research on Elementary and Middle Schools, Johns Hopkins University.

Mefford, P. E., & Pettegrew, B. S. (1997). Fostering literacy acquisition of students with developmental disabilities: Assisted reading with predictable trade books. *Reading Research and Instruction, 36,* 177–190.

Meisinger, E. B., Schwanenflugel, P. J., Bradley, B. A., & Stahl, S. A. (2004). Interaction quality during partner reading, *Journal of Literacy Research, 36,* 111–140.

Morgan, R. T. (1976). "Paired reading": A preliminary report on a technique for parental tuition for cases of reading deficit. *Child Care, Health and Development, 2,* 13–28.

Morris, D., & Nelson, L. (1992). Supported oral reading with low-achieving second graders. *Reading Research and Instruction, 32*(1), 49–63.

National Reading Panel. (2000). *Report of the National Reading Panel.* Washington, DC: National Institute for child Health and Human Development.

Rasinksi, T. V. (2003). *The fluent reader: Oral reading strategies for building word recognition, fluency, and comprehension.* New York: Scholastic Professional Books.

Samuels, S. J. (2004). Toward a theory of automatic information processing in reading, revisited. In R. B. Ruddell & N. J. Unrau (Eds.), *Theoretical models and processes of reading* (5th ed., pp. 1127–1148). Newark, DE: International Reading Association.

Schneeberg, H. (1977). Listening while reading: A fourth study. *The Reading Teacher, 30,* 629–635.

Simmons, D. C., Fuchs, D., Fuchs, L. S., Hodge, J. P., & Mathes, P. G. (1994). Importance of instructional complexity and role reciprocity to classwide peer tutoring. *Learning Disabilities Research and Practice, 9,* 203–212.

Slavin, R. E., & Madden, N. A. (2000). Research on achievement outcomes of Success for All: A summary and response to critics. *Phi Delta Kappan, 82,* 38–40, 59–66.

Stahl, S. A., & Heubach, K. (2005). Fluency-oriented reading instruction. *Journal of Literacy Research, 37,* 25–60.

Stahl, S. A., Heubach, K., & Crammond, B. (1997). *Fluency oriented reading instruction.* National Reading Research Center, Reading Report No. 79, University of Georgia, Athens, GA.

Strickland, D., Ganske, K., & Monroe, J. (2002). *Supporting struggling readers and writers: Strategies for classroom intervention 3–6.* Portland, ME: Stenhouse.

Topping, K. J., & Lindsay, G. A. (1992). Paired reading: A review of the literature. *Research Papers in Education, 5,* 199–246.

Vaughn, S., Chard, D. J., Bryant, D. P., Coleman, M., Tyler, B., Linan-Thompson, S., et al. (2000). Fluency and comprehension interventions for third-grade students. *Remedial and Special Education, 21,* 325–335.

CHAPTER 4

Creating Opportunities for Comprehension Instruction within Fluency-Oriented Reading

KATHERINE A. DOUGHERTY STAHL

THIS CHAPTER INCLUDES:

- Teaching comprehension as part of the Fluency-Oriented Reading Instruction and Wide Reading approaches.
- Using Fluency-Oriented Reading Instruction and Wide Reading approaches to support new learning from informational text.
- Selecting appropriate narrative and informational texts.

The first principle associated with the original version of Fluency-Oriented Reading Instruction (FORI) and subsequently adopted for the Wide Reading program was that lessons would be comprehension oriented (Stahl, Heubach, & Crammond, 1997). The original developers believed that it was important for novice readers to understand that the purpose of reading is to make meaning, not simply call words. Throughout these programs' evolution, the comprehension component has remained an instructional priority.

Research on the FORI and Wide Reading programs, along with other fluency research, has expanded our knowledge of the interplay between fluency and comprehension. Recent research on reading development seems to indicate that fluency and comprehension may be dependent skills early in the process of reading acquisition, but they become independent after high levels of reading fluency are achieved (Paris, 2005). Correlations between fluency scores and comprehension scores diminish in the third and fourth grades (Paris, Carpenter, Paris, & Hamilton, 2005). In other words, novice readers who struggle to decode words are less likely to understand the text, whereas an independent relation is evident among older students who read fluently but have poor comprehension. Researchers have developed many theories to explain why this relationship between fluent word recognition and comprehension diminishes over time (see Paris, 2005; Paris et al., 2005; Stahl & Hiebert, 2005).

Based on this evidence, it is important to consider developmental influences when planning instruction for novice readers. In this chapter, I discuss some ways in which FORI and Wide Reading (Stahl & Heubach, 2005; Kuhn & Stahl, 2004) can be used as part of a literacy program that incorporates the comprehension and vocabulary recommendations of the National Reading Panel (National Institute of Child Health and Human Development [NICHD], 2000) in mid–late first-grade, second-grade, and third-grade classrooms. Novice readers are likely to be able to read complex texts with the additional support provided by FORI or Wide Reading, but they still require *explicit instruction* in word recognition and fluency. Research indicates that fluency is likely to affect the novice reader's level of comprehension. Over the past 8 years, dozens of second-grade teachers across the nation have successfully used FORI or Wide Reading to provide instructional support for their students.

COMPREHENSION AND FLUENCY: SHARED READING AND GUIDED READING IN THE PRIMARY GRADES

One way in which the fluency instruction presented in this book is unique is that it takes place during shared reading time. *Shared reading* consists, in part, of the teacher reading a text aloud as the children follow along with their eyes on their own copy of the text or, in some cases, a big book or a poster. All children in the class have an opportunity to interact with a common text, thus creating a community experience. By the middle of grade 1 and above, shared reading texts should be grade-level texts that address grade-level themes and curriculum topics. However, such texts can be a bit too challenging for students to read by themselves. I like to call these texts *heavy texts*. Such texts have well-developed plots with universal themes or new content-area concepts and rich vocabulary. They tend to be relatively long, generally 450–650 words, although informational texts may be shorter. Basal literature anthologies typically contain several heavy texts. Award-winning trade books, such as the ones that are Caldecott or Coretta

- Caldecottt Award Winners
- Coretta Scott King Award Winners
- Books by Aliki
- Books by Patricia Polacco
- Books by Chris Van Allsburg

Other Individual Heavy Texts:

Barbour, K. (1990). *Little Nino's pizzeria*. New York: Voyager Books.

Dorros, A., & Kleven E. (1991). *Abuela*. New York: Dutton Children's Books.

Falconer, I. (2000). *Olivia*. New York: Simon & Schuster.

Guback, G. (1994). *Luka's quilt*. New York: Greenwillow Books.

Hoffman, M., & Binch, C. (1991). *Amazing grace*. New York: Dial Books for Young Readers—Penguin.

Howard, E. F., & Ransome, J. (1991). *Aunt Flossie's hats (and crab cakes later)*. New York: Clarion Books.

Levinson, R., & Downing, J. (1993). *Soon, Annala*. London: Orchard Books.

Mora, P., & Colon, R. (1997). *Tomas and the library lady*. New York: Random House.

Siebert, D., & Minor, W. (1989). *Heartland*. New York: Harper Trophy.

Swamp, J., & Printup, E. (1997). *Giving thanks: A Native American good morning message*. New York: Lee & Low Books.

FIGURE 4.1. Examples of heavy texts.

Scott King award winners, are often must-read heavy texts. (See additional examples in Figure 4.1.)

In both FORI and Wide Reading shared reading lessons, the teacher reads the text aloud, the teacher and students discuss the text, and then the students echo-read the teacher's section-by-section read-aloud of the text. Wide Reading also integrates partner reading, and to a lesser extent choral reading, whenever time permits. During FORI, students also choral-read, partner-read, and may listen to the story on tape, before being held accountable for reading the story independently.

I make a contrast between shared reading and *guided reading*. "Guided reading is a context in which a teacher supports each reader's development of effective strategies for processing novel texts at increasingly challenging levels of difficulty" (Fountas & Pinnell, 1996, p. 2). The texts you use in guided reading are typically *gradient texts* (see Figure 4.2). Gradient texts are leveled by difficulty using a set of qualitative criteria that include features of predictability and text format (see Peterson, 1991). In guided reading increasingly difficult texts are selected for a small group of students sharing a common instructional reading level. Ideally, students decode the selected text with 90% accuracy on a first or second read. Because you are likely to meet with multiple groups within your reading block, the texts used for guided reading are often shorter than what you use for shared reading. Based on our research, we believe that exposing students to more words per day and to the range of words found in heavy texts contributes to the accelerated progress typically made by FORI and Wide Reading students (Stahl & Heubach, 2005).

I am not advocating the elimination of guided reading at a student's instructional level. However, a comprehensive literacy program must include a shared literacy experience that incorporates heavy text and opportunities for comprehension strategy instruction, high-level discussions, and student inquiry that accommodates the varied skill levels of the children in your classroom. This approach allows less-skilled readers to experience the benefits of reading heavy texts, such as the growth in vocabulary and the development of comprehension strategies (Stanovich, 1986). The support that is provided during both FORI and Wide Reading makes heavy text accessible to all novice readers, except students reading below primer level (Stahl & Heubach, 2005). In our experience with the FORI and Wide Reading approaches, this component of a literacy program requires 20–45 minutes per day, depending on the day's activity.

COMPREHENSION INSTRUCTION WITHIN THE FORI AND WIDE READING LESSON PLANS

Planning Considerations

The decoding and conceptual demands of each text are unique. Even if you are using a basal reading series that contains preselected vocabulary and a multitude of instructional options, each group of students has its specific strengths and needs. Preview the text for its particular conceptual challenges, difficult-meaning vocabulary, and decoding challenges. Figure 4.3 describes a text preview procedure and considerations for planning instruction. Your curriculum and teaching purposes make it necessary for you to shape the instruction to fit your distinctive setting. Selecting texts that are

A Word about Using Gradient Texts

- Using gradient (leveled) text that decreases in predictability as children increase their knowledge of the alphabetic system is a successful way of meeting *decoding* challenges.

Advantages of Gradient Texts

- Provide opportunities for students to read meaningful text while learning more about the alphabetic system.
- Gradual increase in difficulty enables reading fluency to be maintained.
- Allow for novice readers to orchestrate decoding and reading for meaning.
- Provide student accountability.
- Provide context for coaching.

Disadvantages of Gradient Texts

- Lack of complexity.
- Moderate adherence to story grammar.
- Lack the fodder for comprehension strategy instruction, extensions in research, or student discussions addressing issues associated with critical literacy.

FIGURE 4.2. Gradient texts.

- *Big Ideas*—Decide on the big themes or important concepts conveyed by the text. What types of support and experiences will the students need to acquire these insights? What prior knowledge needs to be activated before reading and then integrated with text information during and after reading? In light of the demands of the text, would it make sense to teach or review particular comprehension strategies? What are the connections to the broader classroom curriculum?

- *Vocabulary*—Select the meaning vocabulary that will be unfamiliar to most students. When and how can it be taught most effectively? Must the word be taught before reading because knowing its meaning is essential for understanding the text and an explanation would disrupt the flow during reading? Is the word likely to be unknown but one for which a brief, child-friendly definition at point-of-contact will suffice? Is it a high-utility word that requires elaborated instruction and practice after reading?

- *Word Recognition*—Who is likely to have difficulty with the demands of decoding the text? How much and what type of support is likely to be needed? Do particular words require decoding attention before reading (irregular words or those well beyond the developmental capabilities of most of the readers)? Do the text demands lend themselves to instruction of some particular word recognition competencies during the word-study component of the literacy block?

FIGURE 4.3. Planning the FORI or Wide Reading comprehension lesson.

part of a cohesive, authentic themed unit will promote both fluency and comprehension because the vocabulary tends to reappear and the concepts build on each other. The lesson snapshots in this chapter come from a series of lessons that were part of a second-grade dinosaur unit in literacy that was associated with the science curriculum unit, "Our Changing Earth." Figure 4.4 provides an overview of the weekly activity frame for FORI, Wide Reading, and schedule modifications for informational text.

Introducing the Text (Day 1 of FORI and Wide Reading)

On day 1 of both approaches, you first need to address the vocabulary deemed necessary before reading (a maximum of two or three words) and provide a brief, targeted prereading discussion to activate prior knowledge. Then read the text aloud expressively to the students. It is important that each child has a copy of a text because the children follow along with the

	General FORI plan	Informational texts
Monday (see description for day 1)	Prereading activities Teacher read-aloud Comprehension discussion Possibly, explicit comprehension strategy instruction	General FORI plan Use a graphic organizer (idea map) to teach macrolevel comprehension, organization of ideas in the text.
Tuesday (see description for day 2)	Echo reading (that incorporates comprehension and vocabulary discussion)	No modifications
Wednesday (see description for day 3)	Choral reading and partner reading	No modifications
Thursday (see description for day 4)	Partner reading Possibly, explicit comprehension strategy instruction	After partner reading, students collaboratively summarize the text's key ideas on a personal idea map.
Friday (see description for day 5)	Extension Possibly, explicit comprehension strategy instruction	Each student uses his or her idea map as an aid to create a booklet about the topic for the class library or for K–1 buddies/classrooms.
	General Wide Reading plan	Informational texts
Monday (see description for day 1)	Prereading activities Teacher read-aloud Comprehension discussion Possibly, explicit comprehension strategy instruction	General Wide Reading plan Use a graphic organizer (idea map) to teach macrolevel comprehension, organization of ideas in the text.
Tuesday (see description for day 2)	Echo reading (that incorporates comprehension and vocabulary discussion) (Option: Partner reading if time permits)	No modifications If students partner-read, they may collaboratively summarize the text's key ideas on a personal idea map.
Wednesday (see description for day 5)	Extension Possibly, explicit comprehension strategy instruction	Each student uses his or her idea map as an aid to create a booklet about the topic for the class library or for K–1 buddies/classrooms.
Thursday (see description for day 2)	Echo reading—second text (that incorporates comprehension and vocabulary discussion) (Option: Partner reading if time permits)	No modifications
Friday (see description for day 2)	Echo reading—third text (that incorporates comprehension and vocabulary discussion) (Option: Partner reading if time permits)	No modifications

FIGURE 4.4. Schedule of instruction.

text during the read-aloud. Your initial reading allows the children to hear a model of fluent reading with appropriate phrasing and to make the connection between the words' spellings and pronunciations. You should also stop and question your students intermittently to monitor for general understanding. After you read the text aloud to students, a discussion of the themes or big ideas should take place. You and your students may want to fill in a graphic organizer that reflects the *text structure* as a way of interactively summarizing the key elements of the text. The day 1 lesson ensures that comprehension is brought to the forefront and makes clear to your students that the construction of meaning is the primary purpose of reading. On day 1, instruction emphasizes *macrolevel comprehension* or comprehension of the overall story. If time allows and if a particular comprehension strategy is helpful in comprehending the text, you may wish to teach it explicitly or review it with your students.

By assuming responsibility for reading the text the first time through, you allow your novice readers to focus their attention on gleaning the meaning of the text. This approach is valuable because evidence suggests that when cognitive energy is being used for labored decoding, fewer cognitive resources are available for the construction of meaning (LaBerge & Samuels, 1974; Paris, 2005; Stanovich, 1980). This finding is particularly relevant for novice readers and struggling readers who still must devote energy and attention to figuring out words.

Echo Reading (Day 2 FORI; Days 2, 4, and 5 Wide Reading)

On day 2, you and your students echo read the text. One of the justifications for echo reading with the whole class is to provide the vocabulary and ongoing comprehension support that most novice readers require when reading a heavy text (Stahl, 2003). During echo reading, you read a section of text (a paragraph, multiple paragraphs, or a page) aloud and the students "echo" read the same section of text after your reading of it. Before moving to the next section of text, you can provide brief point-of-contact vocabulary instruction for meaning vocabulary that might be challenging. You can ask questions and clarify confusing concepts in that particular section of text (*microlevel comprehension*). You might also provide a tip for facilitating easy and automatic word recognition in that section of text ("Let's go back and chunk the word *laboratory*, so that you know how to use that tool when you need to read that word by yourself"). In the following snapshot, the students have just finished echo reading a page of a fictional text, *Big Old Bones: A Dinosaur Tale* (Carrick & Carrick, 1989). This is the story of a 19th-century professor's efforts to construct a dinosaur from unidentified fossilized bones. After echo reading, the students take the text home and read it to their parents.

TEACHER: How do you know that the story took place long ago? Tell me something that you see in the picture that indicates to you that this story took place long ago.

STUDENT 1: Buffalos.

TEACHER: You see some buffalo. What else do you see?

STUDENT 2: The train had to stop for water.

TEACHER: Yes, today trains don't need to stop for water. What else do you see?

STUDENT 3: Riding horses.

TEACHER: Right, you see people riding horses. These are all clues for you that the setting of this story is long ago. Okay, let's echo read the next page. (*Reads passage, followed by students.*) "The professor was taking a stroll with his family when their little dog found a bone. 'Very old,' said the professor examining the bone. 'And very big. I've never seen one like it before.' He decided to stay a few days and explore." Who can tell me what it means when it says that the professor was taking a stroll with his family?

STUDENT 4: That means, probably, that they wants [*sic*] to find a bone.

TEACHER: Do you think they knew that there were bones there when they went off for their stroll?

STUDENT 4: No.

TEACHER: No. So what is the *stroll*? They got off the train and they took a . . .

STUDENT 5: Walk.

TEACHER: Yes, a *stroll* is a slow walk.

Choral Reading and Partner Reading (Day 3 FORI)

It is on day 3 that the FORI and Wide Reading approaches diverge. The FORI approach continues with choral reading on Wednesday (see guidelines for day 3), partner reading on Thursday (see guidelines for day 4), and extension activities on Friday (see guidelines for day 5). The Wide Reading approach, on the other hand, continues with extension activities on Wednesday (described as extension activities on day 5 of FORI), and the echo reading of a second and third text on Thursday and Friday (apply the guidelines for day 2).

On day 3 of FORI, you should lead the students in an expressive choral reading of the text. You and the students read the text together, with you setting the pace and helping the students achieve a complete, accurate, and appropriately paced reading. If time permits, this choral reading can be followed by a partner reading of the text. However, partner reading always occurs on day 4. From a comprehension standpoint, it is important that you emphasize an *expressive* rather than "flat" reading of the text because expressive reading is associated with good comprehension. Listeners tend to use expression as a source of information to help them understand the message (Schreiber, 1987). So, reading the passage expressively helps the children with their comprehension. Further, Miller and Schwanenflugel (2006) found that children who read with expression achieved/displayed higher levels of comprehension as indicated by higher standardized scores on a test of reading comprehension ability. Thus, you can emphasize expressive reading as a way of helping your students comprehend a text's message.

Partner Reading (Day 4 FORI)

On the FORI schedule, partner reading is scheduled for day 4. It is possible that the partner reading experience could be the students' sixth encounter with the text (depending on homework). Repeated readings have been shown to improve word recognition, fluency, and comprehension (e.g., Dowhower, 1987, 1989). Additionally, our student interviews indicate that reading for different purposes and in different ways prevents the boredom that might be expected when performing repeated readings. Particularly for struggling readers, the skills that they have gained through all the repeated readings up to this point have built the self-confidence that they can, indeed, participate as full members of their literacy community.

Typically by days 4 and 5, all students using the FORI approach can read the story with a reasonable degree of fluency (Kuhn & Schwanenflugel, 2006; Stahl & Heubach, 2005). As a result, there is often time for a comprehension strategy lesson (National Institute of Child Health and Human Development, 2000) or an *elaborated vocabulary lesson* (see Beck, McKeown, & Kucan, 2002) related to the text. Accordingly, partner reading on day 4 may be directly tied to goals for comprehension instruction. As a classroom teacher, I frequently used partner reading sessions on day 4 as a time for students to hone recently taught comprehension strategies, such as student-generated questioning or taking stock (summarization). As stated earlier, the guided reading texts that I was using for my students with a first- or second-grade instructional reading level simply did not have the complexity of ideas required for this kind of instruction. The lesson snapshot below demonstrates how second-grade students reading *Big Old Bones: A Dinosaur Tale* (Carrrick & Carrick, 1989) used reciprocal questioning during partner reading (also see Figure 4.5). It is worth noting that this was only the second time that these students had independently engaged in questioning each other.

- *Partner 1*: Reads a page or two facing pages.
- *Partner 2*: Generates a question about the section of text read by Partner 1.
- *Partner 1*: Answers the question and identifies the kind of question based on Raphael's (1986) question–answer relationship (QAR). The four relationship categories are Right There, Think and Search, Author and Me, and On My Own. Answers to Right There questions are usually found explicitly in a single sentence or two of the text. Think and Search answers are explicit but must be put together from different sections of the text. A reader needs to use personal experience and information in the text to answer an Author and Me question. On My Own answers are not found in the story but are derived from the reader's personal experience and attitudes. Each of the four question–answer categories are written on a different popsicle stick. Partner 1 identifies the QAR by turning over the corresponding popsicle stick.
- *Partner 2*: Reads the next page or two facing pages.
- *Partner 1*: Generates a question from one of the remaining three types of questions that are still facing up.
- *Partner 2*: Turns the popsicle stick face down that identifies the question type and answers the question.

Note. Summarization practice might proceed in a similar fashion, with the nonreading partner summarizing the section of text that his or her partner just read aloud.

FIGURE 4.5. Using question–answer relationships during partner reading.

STUDENT 1: (*reading*) "Long ago when the old west was new, Professor Potts and his family were traveling across the country. Before their train reached the Rocky Mountains, it stopped for water."

STUDENT 2: When did this story start?

STUDENT 1: Back in the olden days.

STUDENT 2: (*reading*) "The professor was taking a stroll with his family when their little dog found a bone. 'Very old,' said the professor examining the bone. 'And very big. I've never seen one like it before.' He decided to stay a few days and explore."

STUDENT 1: Why did he want to stay a few days and explore?

STUDENT 2: 'Cause, 'cause his little dog found a big bone.

STUDENT 1: (*reading*) "The professor dug until he had collected a large pile of bones. And then, he took them back east to his laboratory. The professor studied all the books in his library, but none of them had bones like these. 'Hmmm,' he said. 'It may be some kind of giant lizard. To know for sure, I'll have to put the bones together.' "

STUDENT 2: Did he find the book that he needed?

STUDENT 1: No.

STUDENT 2: (*reading*) "First, he tried the bones this way. No one would believe an animal like this and too many bones were left over. Then he tried the bones like this. The professor shuddered. 'It gives me bad dreams,' he said. 'Besides the front legs are too small.' "

STUDENT 1: Why does it give him bad dreams?

STUDENT 2: Because it looked so . . . hideous. He just doesn't want to look at it.

Extension Activities (Day 5 FORI or Day 3 Wide Reading)

Day 5 of FORI and day 3 of Wide Reading are allocated as a day for extending the text. Typically in my classroom, students engaged in a conversation group, a writing activity, or a student-generated inquiry project.

Conversation Groups

Many stories and informational texts lend themselves to conversations about themes or issues expressed in the text. The conversational format varies in response to the text. Sometimes it takes the form of an instructional conversation (Saunders & Goldenberg, 1999; Tharp & Gallimore, 1988). Other times, it looks more like collaborative reasoning, with children taking a position and providing evidence for it (Anderson, Chinn, & Waggoner, 2001).

Classroom Snapshot

The Story of Ruby Bridges (Coles & Ford, 1995) tells the true story of the challenges faced by the solitary 6-year-old African American girl attending a New Orleans elementary school after court-ordered desegregation in 1960. After reading *The Story of Ruby Bridges*, the second graders participated in a discussion web (Alverman, 1992) and reflected on two positions: (1) Ruby's family did the right thing in striving for an ideal, and (2) ideals are important, but Ruby's family made a bad decision in putting her in a dangerous, scary, and lonely situation. With a partner, students jotted down reasons that supported each position. Two groups of partners became a group of four. Each person shared at least one idea, and the group came up with a group conclusion for one position or the other. Each group gave a 3-minute class presentation stating their conclusion and justifications for arriving at that conclusion.

Heavy texts are essential for introducing the themes and issues that are critical to a meaningful, concept-driven conversation. Without the scaffolding provided by FORI or Wide Reading, most primary students would be unable to read the texts that provide the springboard for these conversations. We have found that the students who struggle with decoding and writing often have deep insights to share in a conversation about the text. Further, other students that struggle with reading comprehension benefit from hearing their peers share their thinking process surrounding a text.

Writing

As stated in Chapter 2, a comprehensive literacy curriculum should have additional time devoted to the writing process. FORI requires 20–45 minutes per day. In most schools, anywhere from 45 minutes to 1½ or 2 hours of time would remain for other components of the literacy/language arts program. The writing on day 5 might be a short written response to the text or it might be an extended text-related composition that is part of the students' writing process instruction.

For example, after reading the photographic essay *Nature Spy* (Rotner & Kreisler, 1992) with my class, each of my second graders wrote a multiple-sentence caption for the photograph that they had taken earlier in the week during a nature walk. Each photograph and caption became part of a collective photographic essay that was similar to *Nature Spy* and other photographic essays that were part of our class library. Although the photographs had been taken during a different time slot than the literacy period, the captions were constructed during the 30-minute day 5 FORI block.

I took a very different approach to writing during our "Sharing Our Lives" unit. Students read *Aunt Flossie's Hats (and Crabcakes Later)* (Howard & Ransome, 1991), *Chicken Sunday* (Polacco, 1992), and other books with a family memory theme. Each student was responsible for creating a personal narrative describing a family story or memory. This writing project lasted 2 weeks. First, students engaged in a prewriting oral storytelling that described the family memory. Questions and feedback from peers provided the storyteller with helpful information about how to make the story more comprehensible to an audience that was unfamiliar with it. Next, the students wrote drafts of their stories, then revised, edited, and published their final versions. Each child's final version was published next to his or her favorite family recipe in a class cookbook that went home as a

Mother's Day gift. Although we worked on this story during our writer's workshop, we also used our day 5 FORI time block.

Inquiry Projects

What do extended inquiry projects have to do with fluency and comprehension? I found that such projects promote engagement and wide, independent, outside reading that contain common vocabulary and concepts. Writing in the projects tends to reinforce students' familiarity with themed vocabulary and promote fluency when encountering the terminology in novel texts; both of these benefits can be seen in my students' extension activity below.

On day 5 of the *Big Old Bones: A Dinosaur Tale* lesson strand, students worked on their independent inquiry projects. We spent 3 weeks studying about "Our Changing Earth." Each student generated his or her own question related to "Our Changing Earth." Descriptive reports on particular dinosaurs were not acceptable. Some student questions related to plants or animals that lived during particular prehistoric periods, geological features of the earth during particular periods, or prehistoric animals with existing relatives today. (Amazingly, I did this activity for 4 years and the controversy of intelligent design never arose!)

The projects also enabled struggling readers to be a part of a literate community and to view themselves (and to have their peers view them) as researchers with a unique expertise. I taught in a high poverty school. Although some students needed a great deal of support in conducting their research, everyone was able to display an exhibit at our dinosaur museum. Other first- and second-grade classrooms visited the museum. Each junior researcher explained his or her exhibit to the visitors. Project assessments were conducted using the rubric in Figure 4.6.

USING FORI AND WIDE READING
WITH INFORMATIONAL TEXTS

The defining purpose of *informational text* is to convey information (Weaver & Kintsch, 1991). Informational text is structurally different from *narrative text*. In informational text there is usually a hierarchy of ideas and a specification of the type of connections between ideas (Meyer & Rice, 1984; Weaver & Kintsch, 1991). There are several models of expository structures, but most classification systems identify the following five types:

1. Description/collection
2. Sequential

_____ Reading

- You were able to read the information that you displayed.
- Your project accurately reflects information read in at least two different sources.
- You listed at least two references.

_____ Writing

- Your writing and visuals reflect time and effort.
- Your writing mechanics are formal and correct.
- You used your own words; not copied, not plagiarized.

_____ Speaking

- Your oral presentation demonstrated knowledge of topic.
- You presented expert demeanor.

_____ Listening

- You listened respectfully to other presentations.
- You asked questions during other presentations.

FIGURE 4.6. Project rubric.

From *Fluency in the Classroom*, edited by Melanie R. Kuhn and Paula J. Schwanenflugel. Copyright 2008 by The Guilford Press. Permission to photocopy this figure is granted to purchasers of this book for personal use only (see copyright page for details).

3. Cause–effect
4. Problem–solution
5. Compare–contrast

These organizational structures influence the reader's ability to integrate prior knowledge about a topic with new ideas in the text. Text structure awareness also influences the reader's ability to remember the text.

Some evidence suggests that causal or sequential text may not place such a heavy cognitive burden on the reader because it propels itself. In our work with second-grade students, we developed a modified lesson for informational texts with a description/collection structure. Texts with this structure have a series of key ideas, often cued with bold headings, that are followed by supporting details. We provided teachers with protocols for explicit instruction of this common text structure. Figure 4.7 provides a sample weekly instructional protocol for the text *Soil* (Wong, 2001). See also the modified lesson schedule for informational texts in Figure 4.4.

Monday

BEFORE READING THE TEXT ALOUD TO THE STUDENTS:

Tell the students, "Look through this book before I read it to you."

Ask the students, "Do you see any clues about how the ideas in this book might be organized?" "How do you know?" Students should be aware of the table of contents and the headings as keys to organization.

"How do these headings help us as readers?" [Students should indicate that each heading helps the reader prepare for reading that section of text; that is, it tells the reader what he or she will be reading about. That way, the reader can connect new information on the page with what he or she already knew about the topic, and it helps the reader remember the information. When retelling or trying to remember what was read, the headings can help the reader remember the information. After students have provided some of this information, the teacher fills in any missing information about the role of headings.]

DURING TEACHER READ-ALOUD:

Read *Soil* to the students and thoroughly discuss the ideas in each section. The ideas in this text are complex. Remind the students that organizing the information by topic will help them understand more deeply and remember more of the information in the book.

AFTER TEACHER READ-ALOUD:

"Now let's use this idea map to help us group our ideas. (*Point to the graphic.*) What do you think we should put at the top of each box on our idea map to help us organize our ideas and the information we just read?" [Hopefully, students will suggest using book headings as organizing ideas. Again, two of these text sections are quite lengthy. Students will need to know how to identify key ideas and summarize.] "Let's put our first heading, 'What is soil?' at the top of our first box. What general information can you tell me about 'What is soil'?" [The layer of dirt that covers earth/land is called soil. There are different kinds of soil.]

"What shall we put at the top of our next box?" [Discuss with the children that either heading might come next because this is not a sequential text.] "If we choose to put 'Who needs soil?' as our second heading, what important supporting details need to go under that heading? You may need to think-aloud in order to support a summarization of the ideas." [Plants get food and water from soil. Animals and people need soil, because they eat plants that grow in soil.]

"What heading goes in the third box?" [How is soil made?] "What is the most important information that describes how soil is made? If necessary, use a think-aloud to complete the summarization process." [Soil is made from pieces of rock that break apart over a very long time. Those pieces of rock get mixed together with dead animals, plants, and leaves that rotted and broke apart into very small pieces over a very long time.]

CLOSURE

"How did the table of contents and headings help you today? Let's use our headings to help quickly do a retelling of this book. Great!"

(continued)

FIGURE 4.7. Teaching protocol for informational text: *Soil* (Wong, 2001).

Tuesday
Echo reading and comprehension questions.

Wednesday
Choral reading and partner reading.

Thursday
After partner reading *Soil*: Distribute the idea map and discuss what headings should be used at the top of each box. (If the children have not learned summarization skills, they will get frustrated trying to put all of the information in the three boxes.)

"I would like you to complete your own idea map with your partner. Talk about the map together, but each of you has your own copy for recording the information. Organize the big ideas of our book using your idea map. Remember that the heading is your big idea. Generate a heading and information for each box on the idea map." [Headings should be accepted in any order. This is not a sequential text.] "You should write the heading, underline it, and add information on your idea map. You and your partner will need to decide on the headings and the information that will go in all three boxes."

Collect the idea maps at the end of the session.

Friday
Redistribute each idea map. Ask students to turn to a partner and share what they know about soil, using their idea map to help them remember. Next have them independently write a book for your class library/younger students about soil. Distribute the book frames and review the format with the students. They may use their idea map to help them organize their books. Encourage the students to use their own words, to write complete sentences, and to add information that they learned in science. After they have finished writing their book, they may go back and illustrate it. (We have found that illustrating before the book is finished takes time away from writing.)

FIGURE 4.7. (*continued*)

Before reading the text on day 1, teachers explicitly taught the text structure. After reading the text, teachers employed a graphic organizer (idea map) to visually represent and structure the collaborative retelling of the text information. This idea map was completed collaboratively as a class. Each idea map had spaces for the organizational headings used in the texts and room to record supporting details. After partner reading on day 4 (FORI), students completed their own idea maps that corresponded with the informational texts they were reading. This activity could also be incorporated into day 2 or 3 in the Wide Reading format. On day 5 (FORI) or day 3 (Wide Reading), students created books that presented the information on the topic about which they had read that week.

Students read *Soil* (Wong, 2001) during the classroom literacy block. It had challenging vocabulary and concepts. However, the concurrent science unit was also related to soil. Each afternoon, students encountered the same vocabulary in their science books, engaged in hands-on science activities, and wrote about the results of experiments. The cohesiveness of the classroom curriculum fostered fluency, vocabulary development, concept development, and reading comprehension.

CLOSING THOUGHTS

As a teacher in primary classrooms (grades 1, 2, and 3), the application of FORI and Wide Reading changed the way I taught literacy and my expectations about student abilities. I still provided instruction in word recognition, guided reading with instructional-level texts, and writing workshop. However, implementing fluency-oriented instruction during shared reading enabled me to develop a vocabulary and comprehension component that had never been possible in my work with novice readers. Literacy instruction became authentic, cohesive, and purposeful. Reading fluency improved, but students did not adopt the race-through-the-text reading that is often the result of deliberate efforts to improve reading rate. Rate and expressiveness improved as the students became "code breakers, meaning makers, text users and text critics" (Muspratt, Luke, & Freebody, 1997).

REFERENCES

Alvermann, D. E. (1992). The discussion web: A graphic aid for learning across the curriculum. *The Reading Teacher, 45*, 92–99.

Anderson, R. C., Chinn, C. A., & Waggoner, M. A. (2001). Patterns of discourse in two kinds of literature discussion. *Reading Research Quarterly, 36*, 378–411.

Beck, I. L., McKeown, M. G., & Kucan, L. (2002). *Bringing words to life: Robust vocabulary instruction*. New York: Guilford Press.

Carrick, C., & Carrick, D. (1989). *Big old bones: A dinosaur tale*. New York: Houghton Mifflin.

Coles, R., & Ford, G. (1995). *The story of Ruby Bridges*. New York: Scholastic.

Dowhower, S. L. (1987). Effects of repeated reading on second-grade transitional readers' fluency and comprehension. *Reading Research Quarterly, 22*, 389–406.

Dowhower, S. (1989). Repeated reading: Theory into practice. *The Reading Teacher, 42*, 502–507.

Fountas, I. C., & Pinnell, G. S. (1996). *Guided reading: Good first teaching for all children*. Portsmouth, NH: Heinemann.

Howard, E. F., & Ransome, J. (1991). *Aunt Flossie's hats (and crabcakes later)*. New York: Clarion.

Kuhn, M., & Schwanenflugel, P. (2006). Fluency-Oriented Reading Instruction: A merging of theory and practice. In K. A. D. Stahl & M. C. McKenna (Eds.),

Reading research at work: Foundations of effective practice (pp. 205–213). New York: Guilford Press.

Kuhn, M., & Stahl, K. (2004). *Teaching manual: The development of fluent and automatic reading.* Unpublished manuscript.

LaBerge, D., & Samuels, S. A. (1974). Toward a theory of automatic information processing in reading. *Cognitive Psychology, 6,* 293–323.

Meyer, B. J. F., & Rice, G. E. (1984). The structure of text. In P. D. Pearson, R. Barr, P. Mosenthal, & M. Kamil (Eds.), *Handbook of reading research* (Vol. I, pp. 319–352). White Plains, NY: Longman.

Miller, J., & Schwanenflugel, P. J. (2006). Prosody of syntactically complex sentences in the oral reading of young children. *Journal of Educational Psychology, 98,* 839–843.

Muspratt, S., Luke, A., & Freebody, P. (1997). *Constructing critical literacies.* Cresskills, NJ: Hampton.

National Institute of Child Health and Human Development (NICHD). (2000). *Report of the National Reading Panel. Teaching children to read: An evidence-based assessment of the scientific research literature on reading and its implications for reading instruction* (NIH Publication No. 00-4769). Washington, DC: U.S. Government Printing Office. Available at www.nationalreading-panel.org.

Paris, S. G. (2005). Re-interpreting the development of reading skills. *Reading Research Quarterly, 40,* 184–202.

Paris, S. G., Carpenter, R. D., Paris, A. H., & Hamilton, E. E. (2005). Spurious and genuine correlates of children's reading comprehension. In S. G. Paris & S. A. Stahl (Eds.), *Children's reading comprehension and assessment* (pp. 131–160). Mahwah, NJ: Erlbaum.

Peterson, B. (1991). Selecting books for beginning readers. In D. E. DeFord, C. A. Lyons, & G. S. Pinnell (Eds.), *Bridges to literacy: Learning from Reading Recovery* (pp. 119–147). Portsmouth, NH: Heinemann.

Polacco, P. (1992). *Chicken Sunday.* New York: Philomel Books.

Raphael, T. (1986). Teaching question–answer relationships, revisited. *The Reading Teacher, 39,* 516–522.

Rotner, S., & Kreisler, K. (1992). *Nature spy.* New York: Macmillan.

Saunders, W. M., & Goldenberg, C. (1999). Effects of instructional conversations and literature logs on limited- and fluent-English-proficient students' story comprehension and thematic understanding. *Elementary School Journal, 99,* 279–301.

Schreiber, P. A. (1987). Prosody and structure in children's syntactic processing. In R. Horowitz & S. J. Samuels (Eds.), *Comprehending oral and written language* (pp. 243–270). San Diego, CA: Academic Press.

Stahl, K. A. D. (2003). *The effects of three instructional methods on the reading comprehension and content acquisition of novice readers.* Unpublished doctoral dissertation, University of Georgia, Athens, GA.

Stahl, S. A., & Heubach, K. M. (2005). Fluency-Oriented Reading Instruction. *Journal of Literacy Research, 37,* 25–60.

Stahl, S. A., Heubach, K., & Crammond, B. (1997). *Fluency-Oriented Reading Instruction* (Reading research report no. 79). Athens, GA and College Park, MD: National Reading Research Center.

Stahl, S. A., & Hiebert, E. H. (2005). The "word factors": A problem for reading comprehension assessments. In S. G. Paris & S. A. Stahl (Eds.), *Current issues in reading comprehension and assessment* (pp. 161–186). Mahwah, NJ: Erlbaum.

Stanovich, K. E. (1980). Toward an interactive–compensatory model of individual differences in the development of reading fluency. *Reading Research Quarterly, 16,* 32–71.

Stanovich, K. E. (1986). Matthew effects in reading: Some consequences of individual differences in the acquisition of literacy. *Reading Research Quarterly, 21,* 360–407.

Tharp, R. G., & Gallimore, R. (1988). *Rousing minds to life: Teaching, learning and schooling in social context.* Cambridge, UK: Cambridge University Press.

Weaver, C. A. III, & Kintsch, W. (1991). Expository text. In P. D. Pearson (Ed.), *Handbook of reading research* (Vol. 1, pp. 230–245). White Plains, NY: Longman.

Wong, G. (2001). *Soil.* Washington, DC: National Geographic.

CHAPTER 5

Motivating the Development of Reading Fluency

MATTHEW QUIRK

THIS CHAPTER INCLUDES:

- Understanding the characteristics of a motivated reader.
- Understanding motivation to read as a system of interrelated parts.
- Understanding the relationship between motivation to read and reading fluency skill development.
- Strategies and tools for teachers to improve students' motivation to read.

Many elementary school teachers struggle with the question of how to motivate their students to learn to read. Given that you are reading this chapter, perhaps you are one of them. In fact, research has confirmed that teachers struggle with a number of motivational issues, including how to create more interest in reading, how to increase the amount and breadth of their students' reading, and how to develop an *intrinsic* (internal) desire for reading in their students that will serve them well throughout their school careers and the rest of their lives (O'Flahavan, Gambrell, Guthrie, Stahl, & Alvermann, 1992). Teachers' motivational questions and concerns are rooted in their intuitive understanding that motivated students also tend to be those who seek out more opportunities to read, persist when they encounter difficulty with reading, and are more actively engaged in literacy instruction—all of which contribute to increased reading skill. This chapter focuses on how *motivation* to read impacts the development of reading fluency in young children as well as how the development of reading fluency can, in turn, impact students' motivation to read. However, it should be apparent that much of the motivational theory discussed in this chapter is relevant to reading development throughout a child's academic career.

WHAT MAKES A "MOTIVATED READER"?

Before beginning a discussion of how motivation and reading fluency are related, it is important to establish exactly what is meant when I use the term *motivated reader*. All teachers can identify students in their classes who seem motivated to read, along with others who are reluctant to engage in reading activities. Unfortunately, as with many issues related to reading development, there is no universally agreed-upon set of characteristics that differentiates a motivated reader from a reluctant one. There are, however, some core characteristics that most of us would agree are present in motivated readers—or, in some cases, characteristics that are lacking in reluctant readers. These core characteristics serve as the foundation for my discussion on the ways in which motivation and the development of reading fluency are related to one another.

Motivation to read is multifaceted; in other words, it is comprised of a conglomerate of interrelated factors (Wigfield, 1997). Because a comprehensive examination of all of the constructs and influences that make up a student's motivation to read is beyond the scope of this chapter, I focus my discussion on the three areas that I feel are the most important to the relationship between motivation to read and the development of reading fluency: *reading self-efficacy, value for reading,* and *goals for reading.* Not coincidentally, these are also areas where you, as a teacher, can have a significant impact on your students' motivation—both through your choice of classroom materials and through the procedures you implement during daily reading instructional time. The following discussion describes the research in these three areas by explaining how they are related to your students' overall motivation to read and how motivation impacts the reading behaviors you may see in your classrooms everyday.

Reading Self-Efficacy

Self-efficacy is defined as "people's judgments of their capabilities to organize and execute courses of action required to attain designated types of performances" (Bandura, 1986, p. 391). In other words, your sense of self-efficacy comes from a personal assessment of your own ability to accomplish a task—and with what degree of success—or your sense of "I can do it." People's sense of self-efficacy has been shown to influence a variety of behaviors, including what activities they choose to engage in (*choice*), how hard they are willing to work (*effort*), and how long they are willing to persist when they are having difficulty (*persistence*). In the case of reading, these behaviors hold obvious implications for the development of fluency (Bandura, 1986; Locke & Latham, 1990; Weiner, 1985). People who have low self-efficacy for a given task tend to put forth little effort or avoid it altogether, whereas those who feel capable are more likely to actively participate and persist in the face of difficulty (Schunk, 1991). Because fluency development is dependent upon learners spending a great deal of time reading connected text, self-efficacy can significantly impact its development.

Research specifically addressing children's reading self-efficacy has found that the confidence that children have in their ability to successfully complete reading-related tasks has a significant impact on the amount of reading they engage in, the types of books that they choose to read, and the level of persistence they put forth when confronted with challenging texts (Wigfield & Guthrie, 1997)—all of which hold implications for the development of their reading fluency. For example, young students who are very motivated readers are more likely than reluctant readers to choose books that push their skills to the limit. Practicing with books that are at these children's instructional level—or even close to their frustration level—would push them to become more strategic in navigating text, expose them to a wider variety of unfamiliar words, and improve their word identification skills—all of which should improve their reading fluency. On the other hand, reluctant readers would be more likely to choose books that are at or below their independent reading level. They might be more likely to choose predictable or decodable texts that are less likely to push them to improve their word identification skills and strategies and which would fail to contribute to their growth in reading fluency. A list of questions that you can ask yourself to reflect on your students' reading self-efficacy can be found in Figure 5.1.

Value for Reading

In order for your learners to be motivated, it is also necessary for them to perceive some value in participating in reading activities. *Value for reading* can be established at a number of different levels. In fact, research has found that people place value on various tasks or activities at three different levels: *interest value, attainment value,* and *utility value* (Eccles et al., 1983). In relation to reading, *interest value* would be defined as how much an individual likes or is interested in reading or in a particular reading activity. Does he or she like partner reading? Does he or she look forward to reading a favorite book? *Attainment value* pertains to the perceived importance of doing well in reading, which is often influenced by how much those around you value reading. Does the child see family members,

1. Do my students choose challenging books when given the opportunity to self-select reading materials?

2. Do my students have more than one or two strategies that they feel comfortable using when trying to decode unfamiliar words?

3. Do my students believe that they are capable of becoming better readers with effort?

4. Are my students aware of their own individual growth in reading (even if this growth is considered "below grade level")?

5. Are there things that I, as the teacher, could do to help my students become more strategic, for example, help them self-select books that are developmentally appropriate/interesting and/or help them become more aware of their individual progress, thereby improving their self-confidence in reading?

FIGURE 5.1. Questions for teachers to use when reflecting on students' reading self-efficacy.

teachers, and other adults and children in his or her surrounding community reading books and newspapers? Do these people talk about how important it is to read? Finally, *utility value* is the child's perceived usefulness for reading or for becoming a better reader. This type of value can be translated into the questions, "How can I use this skill to accomplish something that is important to me?" and "How can I use reading to find out something that I want to know?" Value for reading is an area of a child's motivation that can easily be overlooked due to the fact that reading is such an integral part of the educational process and the value placed on literacy seems obvious to those who have spent most of their lives involved in education at one level or another. However, some children in today's classrooms come from households and communities that may not place the same value on literacy and do not model literate behaviors for their children on a daily basis; this disparity between home and school values can be a source of confusion when children spend a significant part of each school day reading or learning to read without a true understanding of how these skills could be used in their daily lives.

My experience with teaching reluctant second-grade readers has exposed me to the ways in which some children hold a very surface level value on reading, without truly understanding how reading could allow them to do things about which they really care. These are the type of students who will tell any adult that they understand reading is important, yet they may not have made the personal connection with reading that might motivate them to read beyond what is required by a teacher or parent.

For example, when I asked a group of my second-grade students, "Why is reading important to you?", their typical response was, "So I can do well in school."

My immediate follow-up was, "Well, why is doing well in school important?"

This, in turn, was met with answers such as, "So I can get a job and make money to live!" or "So my parents won't get mad at me!"

Although these responses may seem to show an adequate understanding of the value in reading, it is not the type of response that shows the level of value needed for a second grader (or any student, for that matter) to get really excited about reading. Your students need to connect to reading as a tool they can use to reach personally relevant and important goals in their daily lives. They need to see how reading can be used in authentic situations rather than just as a skill needed to get through their basal anthology every day. When children recognize this type of value in reading, they are likely to read more both in and out of school. As noted elsewhere, this reading practice has direct implications on the development of their reading fluency, as well as many other requisite reading skills. Figure 5.2 suggests ways in which you can communicate the value of reading to these students.

Goals for Reading

The third area of motivational research that I feel is important for fluency is *goals for reading*. Academic goals are most commonly discussed in two ways. First, are your students setting goals for their learning and monitoring their progress toward reaching those goals? And second, what do your students use as a point of reference when judging their level of performance in reading or reading-related activities (their goal orientation)? As a teacher, you can have a profound impact on both of these areas and thereby help your students improve their reading skill. Of course, with improved reading skill, your students will also likely experience more general success in school across the curriculum.

Encouraging your students to set goals for their reading development is important for many reasons. First, by setting goals, your students establish clear expectations toward which they are working. Both you and your students can use these goals as a benchmark for evaluating their performance (Turner, Husman, & Schallert, 2002). You can also use goals to provide your students with concrete feedback, showing them where they are making progress as well as where more work is needed. As you will see later in this chapter, setting and monitoring goals for the development of reading fluency is relatively easy to do and can be a valuable tool for

1. Help your students see how reading can allow them to achieve goals that they feel are important in their lives (even if *they* seem trivial to you).

2. Model the value that reading has in your daily life. Read the newspaper when they are returning to the classroom after art or physical education. Tell them about the books and magazines that you are reading for enjoyment. Emphasize how reading has helped you achieve some of your personal goals in life. Even if you aren't an avid reader, there are ways that you are using literacy to reach personal goals in life, which is important to share with your students.

3. Learn about your students' interests by using a reading interest inventory at the beginning of the school year. Ask children about their reading interests through the conversations that you have with them in weekly progress monitoring meetings. Bring these interests into your reading instruction.

4. Bring in parents and community members as guest readers to discuss how reading has impacted their lives.

5. Allow time for students to read self-selected books/materials every day, providing them with the support of tapes or CDs or partners, if necessary.

FIGURE 5.2. Communicating to students the value reading can have in their daily lives.

From *Fluency in the Classroom*, edited by Melanie R. Kuhn and Paula J. Schwanenflugel. Copyright 2008 by The Guilford Press. Permission to photocopy this figure is granted to purchasers of this book for personal use only (see copyright page for details).

encouraging your children to focus on their own individual improvement rather than comparing how well they are doing to how their peers are performing. It should be noted that young children are not very good at self-setting academic goals, so you will need to play an instrumental role in scaffolding this process for your students. A detailed explanation of how this goal setting can be done is also described later in this chapter.

Goal-orientation theory focuses on what composes the driving motives behind setting achievement goals. In order to understand the impact of students' goal orientation on their achievement, it is first important to distinguish between *performance* goals and *mastery* goals. Students whose goal orientation is on performance focus on demonstrating superior performance compared with others. For example, students who have a *performance goal orientation* are more often concerned with getting the highest score in the class on a test than with learning where they did well and how they may need to improve. Research has linked performance goals to some negative outcomes, including withdrawal of effort in the face of failure, surface processing of study material, and decreased task enjoyment (Elliot, 1999; Dweck & Leggett, 1988; Nicholls, 1989). Thus, students who hold a predominantly performance goal orientation toward reading would be more likely to avoid reading challenging texts, feel less enjoyment when reading, and be more likely to judge that they lack ability when they encounter difficulty with reading related tasks.

In contrast, students who have a mastery orientation are more likely to focus on their own individual improvement and are less concerned with comparisons to their peers. Children with *mastery goals* believe that exerting some effort leads to success. They prefer more challenging material and are willing to take some risks in their schoolwork by trying something hard and not necessarily choosing a "sure thing." They have what is called an intrinsic (internal) interest in learning (Ames, 1992; Ames & Archer, 1988; Elliot & Dweck, 1988; Weiner, 1979). Therefore, these students would be more likely to read challenging texts, take the chance that a book might be too difficult for them, and feel more genuine enjoyment when reading. All of these outcomes, as noted in other chapters in this book, have implications for the development of reading fluency.

As you are probably realizing at this point, everything that your students and you do during reading instruction can have a significant impact on how they perceive their own individual ability in reading, why reading should be valued, and what it is they should be focusing on to improve their reading skills. Motivation to read is a very complex system with many interrelated components. Changes in one aspect of reading motivation will have implications for others. Figure 5.3 provides a graphic description of these relationships. As you can see in this figure, the three key components of students' motivation to read (reading self-efficacy, value for reading, and reading goals) all influence one another. Taken together, they comprise students' overall motivation to read, which, in turn, influences their reading fluency skill development (and plays a role in determining how much the child reads, the difficulty of texts that he or she chooses to read, etc.). The arrow running from *reading fluency* to *motivation to read* illustrates how children can become more motivated to read as they perceive that they are becoming more skilled readers.

HOW DOES MOTIVATION THEORY APPLY
TO INDIVIDUAL CHILDREN?

Motivational theory is a bit abstract and can be a bit difficult to understand. To get a clearer picture of how these factors work together, I would like to put them into context by discussing how they might impact the development of reading fluency skill using two hypothetical students (based on a composite of students with whom I have worked).

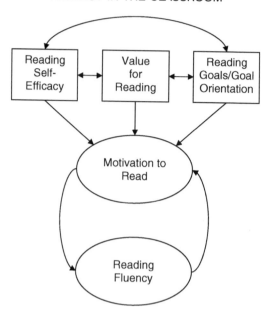

FIGURE 5.3. Interrelationships of motivation to read and reading fluency development.

First let's consider a second grader named George, who is very motivated to read. His nose is constantly in a book, and he is well ahead of his fellow classmates in developing his reading fluency skills. George comes from a home life in which he has always been surrounded by adults who read (*attainment value*). This ongoing exposure introduced him to the many ways that literature could enrich his life and be used to reach personally relevant goals (*utility value*). Thus he naturally developed a strong sense for the *value of reading*. Going back to his first days in prekindergarten, George has always excelled in reading, which has contributed to his high *reading self-efficacy*. Last year, his first-grade teacher's reading instructional approach was heavily influenced by her belief that she should immerse young children in a variety of reading experiences using a number of different genres of authentic literature. This teaching style fit perfectly with George's confidence in his reading abilities and his seemingly never-ending desire to get his hands on different pieces of literature to try them out (*interest value*). Now, as he enters second grade he is still reading well above grade level, yet he continues to work hard at reading because he enjoys being able to explore the world around him through books (*mastery goal orientation*). When George is reading a book in school and comes to a word he doesn't know, he uses a variety of strategies to figure it out. Even when he has difficulty with a book, he knows that with practice he will get through it and eventually read it with ease (*high reading self-efficacy*), which is why George often tries to read books that push his reading skills to their limit (*setting challenging reading goals*). The last time we saw him, his goal was to read the *Harry Potter* series, and he was working on it with his mother.

Now, let's consider another student, Alexandra, in second grade. Like George, Alexandra also comes from a family where reading is thought to be very important; however, she has always struggled in school with reading-related activities, which has had a negative impact on her *reading self-efficacy*. Because of her struggles, Alexandra is always looking for ways to avoid having to read so she will not look "stupid" in front of her peers (*performance goal orientation*). During her class's hour-long reading instruction each morning, Alexandra constantly makes trips to the water fountain, bathroom, and pencil sharpener to get away from the embarrassment and frustration that come with her struggles in reading (*low reading self-efficacy*). When she encounters a word she doesn't know, she immediately tries to sound it out; however, many times this approach does not work and even when it does, reading every word this way becomes a huge burden that makes her tire of reading quickly. Alexandra attributes her difficulties with reading to her low ability, and as a result of repeated failures, sees little hope that things will change no matter how much effort she gives to becoming a better reader (*low reading self-efficacy*). Her lack of confidence is evident when she is given the opportunity to self-select books. She never chooses anything with "too many words"—a choice that further stunts the development of her reading skills. She often chooses predictable texts that she can read successfully; however, she finds these texts boring (*low interest value*). She never sets any goals for improving her reading because she feels as though she will certainly fail; she will not be able to match the performance of the other students in her class. Because she is not good at reading, Alexandra rarely has the opportunity to use reading to accomplish anything that is important or interesting to her (*low utility and interest value*). As a result, she has decided that regardless of what her parents and teachers think, reading is stupid and not something that she would ever choose to do on her own time (*low attainment and utility value*).

As many teachers would agree, it is not uncommon to see students very similar to George and Alexandra, or students that exhibit some of the reading behaviors described in the above scenarios. The one area in which George and Alexandra are most different is in their *reading self-efficacy*. George's high reading self-efficacy enables him to seek out books that challenge his reading abilities. Because he is able to choose books that are challenging, George often selects books based on personal interest, with little regard for how difficult it may be for him to read. George's experiences with high-interest texts reinforce his family's belief that reading is important and should be used daily, as George tries to do by picking up a book whenever he can. This habit gives him the repeated practice he needs to continue improving his already superior reading fluency skill.

In contrast, Alexandra's reading self-efficacy is particularly low, which comes as no surprise given that she has endured 3 years of repeated failures when asked to complete reading-related activities at school. Unlike George, Alexandra only reads what the teacher requires, and she has actually become increasingly skilled at finding ways to avoid the required reading as well. Alexandra can feel her parents' uneasiness over her struggles through their constant reminders of the importance of reading. As a self-preservation mechanism, Alexandra has decided that reading is not important and that she doesn't really need it anyway—a stance that only compounds the problem of getting her to practice reading. Alexandra rarely read and is well aware of the fact that she is falling behind most of her peers, still struggling to use word-by-word reading to get through books at the end of her second grade year. George, meanwhile, continues to gain confidence in his reading ability due to the fact that he rarely encounters a book that gives him difficulty and actually sees difficult books as a fun and exciting challenge. The implications that these varying dispositions have on George's and Alexandra's fluency development over the course of their second-grade year are obvious, given the importance of wide reading and repeated practice for developing word identification strategies, automaticity, and overall reading fluency.

George and Alexandra represent extreme examples from both ends of the motivational spectrum. It is likely that most of your students fall somewhere along the continuum in-between those two extremes. Whatever students' motivational dispositions, there are many strategies that you can implement to improve your students' reading self-efficacy and value for reading, as well as help them learn to set goals for their reading development by focusing on their individual progress and downplaying any comparisons with their peers. Importantly, all of these factors also contribute to improved reading fluency.

HOW DOES MOTIVATION TO READ IMPACT READING FLUENCY DEVELOPMENT?

The basis for understanding how reading motivation impacts the development of reading fluency is probably best addressed by what is commonly known in the field of reading education as *Matthew effects* (Stanovich, 1986). The term *Matthew effects* refers to the finding that the gap in skill level between good and poor readers widens as poor readers avoid reading whereas skilled readers engage in additional opportunities to read. As good readers continue to gain reading skill through extra practice, the skill level of poor readers tends to stagnate because these children avoid involvement in reading-related tasks. The differences between these groups are best illustrated by the results of a research study conducted by Anderson, Wilson, and Fielding (1988), which found that good readers read approximately five times as many minutes per day as average readers and nearly 200 times as many minutes per day as poor readers. As you can see, over the course of an entire year (or in many cases, multiple years), these differences begin to add up. Because fluency is a skill that develops over years of repeated practice and through the mastery of numerous prerequisite reading skills, students' level of motivation will impact how often they seek out opportunities to read and how rapidly they are able to develop into a fluent reader.

Beyond the impact that children's motivation to read can have on the sheer amount of reading they choose to do during and after school, motivation also directly effects how engaged students are during fluency-building activities, such as those described throughout this book. Again, degree of engagement holds obvious implications for the effectiveness of these activities in improving students' reading fluency. Some of these activities might not be inherently motivating for some students; they require that students "follow along" while the teacher is reading and while their partner is reading, and that they engage in some independent reading after school. As many of you would agree, this can be a lot to expect of some primary-grade students. Nevertheless, teacher's can get children excited about reading by using high-interest materials and by displaying enthusiasm about the process. Luckily, as Chapter 2 notes, evoking enthusiasm is much easier if grade-level materials can be used because they are more complex and present a range of often new and interesting concepts. Further, you can give explicit examples of how these fluency activities have improved your students' ability to reach personally relevant goals through reading.

HOW DOES THE DEVELOPMENT OF READING SKILLS IMPACT THE MOTIVATION TO READ?

Whereas motivation to read can have a clear impact on the development of reading fluency, fluency development can, in turn, affect motivation. That is, it is possible to utilize students' improving skills to bolster their motivation to read. To illustrate how this process works, I would like for you to think back to any new skill you have developed in the recent past (e.g., golfing, playing chess, learning to sail). In the beginning, you were probably a bit reluctant to take risks and most likely hit some points of frustration where you began asking yourself if this new skill were really worth all of the time and energy you were putting into learning it. Young children who struggle with learning to read most likely hit similar points during their early elementary years. Now, if you stuck with it, remember that moment when you began to realize that you were actually showing some signs of improvement, whether it was a par you made on a golf hole, beating your mentor in a game of chess, or successfully rigging your sailboat without the help of your instructor? It is a very empowering feeling that most likely motivated you to begin practicing even more; a chain reaction is set in motion whereby increased amounts of practice lead to more rapid skill development, further fueling your motivation to continue practicing.

Although little research has been done to examine whether this same chain reaction actually occurs in classroom situations, it has been our experience that when children realize they are capable of improvement and they see their hard work leading to the attainment of personally relevant goals, the realization can have a very positive impact on their motivation to continue working hard. For example, in a recent study we trained teachers to hold monthly "goal-setting conferences," wherein students and teachers worked together to develop goals for students' reading fluency development as well as to monitor the progress being made toward goals that were set in previous conferences (a more detailed description of the procedures for these conferences is explained later in this chapter). At the end of the year, teachers reported a variety of positive outcomes from these conferences, including the improvement of students' self-evaluation skills, improvement in their ability to set moderately difficult learning goals, and an increase in their awareness of the progress that was being made through their efforts and hard work.

Thinking back to my second graders who were reluctant readers provides an example of how this relationship can play itself out in the area of reading. At the beginning of the year, these children had had very few positive experiences with reading, which resulted in a low reading self-efficacy for many of them. They did not believe they were capable of becoming better readers, regardless of how hard they worked. However, as the year progressed, their skills did improve. I made it a point to look back regularly at the stories that children had trouble reading at the beginning of the year and compare them with the stories that they had recently completed. This is a simple and powerful 5-minute weekly activity that really focused the students' attention on the fact that they were improving, and it seemed to validate the hard work that they were putting in each morning during their reading class. By the end of the year, students who couldn't get through a primer passage in September were coming into my class carrying challenging books such as *Charlotte's Web* that they had checked out of the library earlier that morning. Although they may not have been able to read the book independently, the fact that they were excited to show me a self-selected book that indicated they were tackling more difficult texts was proof to me of the strides they had made, both in skill level *and* motivation to read.

HOW CAN I INTEGRATE MOTIVATION TECHNIQUES INTO FLUENCY INSTRUCTION AND ASSESSMENT?

Recent research suggests that improving students' motivation to read, with students as young as second grade, has a direct effect on the development of their reading fluency skill (Quirk, 2005). Thus, I would like to turn your attention to a few general strategies and classroom practices (some of which I have alluded to throughout this chapter) that you can utilize within the fluency building techniques outlined in this book to improve students' motivation to read.

Although we have recently discovered that the Wide Reading of text with appropriate scaffolding is an effective approach to fluency instruction, much fluency-oriented reading instruction focuses on getting students to read a text repeatedly. This approach to building fluency is predicated on research suggesting that students will become more familiar with the words and text structures they encounter in texts when they are given multiple opportunities to read through them. With this familiarity comes automaticity, which frees up the child's mental resources to focus on higher-order skills such as fluency and comprehension (Logan, 1997). As with anything that requires repeated practice, the more interested the students are in the topic or story line of the book they are reading, the more motivated (due to increased interest value) they will be to engage in the necessary repeated readings that eventually build reading fluency. Therefore, in an ideal situation, children would self-select the books (provided they were challenging) that they will use to practice reading over the course of the week. Although this book emphasizes whole-group instruction, it may be feasible for you to give your students a choice between a few different selections for use as the basis of their whole-class or small-group instruction and then plan the fluency-oriented activities around the book(s) that they select. Alternatively, giving students a choice in reading material may also fit in their independent reading time.

Another strategy that capitalizes on the influence of motivation on skill development (and vice versa) is the use of monthly "fluency progress monitoring" conferences. These conferences require only 5 minutes per student and could be a powerful way to work with your students on setting monthly goals for their reading development. During these conferences, you could assess and track individual student's strengths and needs. You could have students focus on their own individual progress, making them more mastery oriented, and show them concrete examples of how their hard work is translating into improved reading fluency. Moreover, your comments to students during an everyday reading class can be directed at improvements that you have noticed in their oral reading performance, avoiding the temptation to compare them to other children in the class. Specific guidelines and examples for implementing these monthly conferences can be found in Figures 5.4 and 5.5.

Fluency progress monitoring conferences should be conducted with each student individually once a month. Each conference should take approximately 5 minutes and consists of two brief parts. First, you need to administer a curriculum-based assessment (see Chapter 8) or a running record to each student for 1 minute as he or she reads a grade-level passage from the classroom textbooks; you should also determine the number of correct words read per minute from this reading. Alternatively, you can conduct an assessment such as the Dynamic Indicators of Basic Early Literacy Skills or DIBELS "Progress Monitoring" assessments (Good, Simmons, & Smith, 1998), which can be found at www.dibels.uoregon.edu. You can download directions for progress monitoring assessments along with grade-level passages for each month of the school year, and protocols for scoring your evaluation of each student. Included in this packet of materials is an important motivational tool, a bar graph page that allows you and your student to plot his or her fluency scores to determine *reading rate* (expressed as correct words per minute). This graph gives you and your student a simple visual aid that illustrates his or her monthly progress in developing reading fluency over the course of the school year (see the example in Figure 5.5). You might also rate a child's reading expressiveness using the National Assessment of Educational Progress (NAEP) or Rasinski's fluency scale (see Chapter 8) to emphasize the use of prosodic elements and to keep children from viewing their developing fluency as exclusively related to rate. You can then discuss any growth that is evident from the student's previous month's performance (i.e., goals set and reached) and possible reasons for this growth.

Then, in the second part of the 5-minute conference, you should conduct a "goal setting and monitoring" discussion with your student, during which the student is able to set new reading goals as well as check off any previous goals that have been completed. This component of the conference is a great way for you to model how to set academic goals and also how to monitor progress toward goals that have been previously set. In the first few conferences of the year, you should model how to set specific and moderately challenging reading goals, gradually reducing the level of scaffolding you provide each month.

When setting reading goals in the initial conference of the year, you need to take into account each student's reading level along with any individual reading strengths that could potentially be utilized to improve reading fluency. Example goals might include (1) reading with more expression (using a tape-recorded reading to track progress); (2) learning a specific reading skill(s) or strategy that you and your student plan to work on; (3) improving reading rate on a monthly curriculum-based assessment or running record passage; or (4) others on which you and your student agree. In any case, you should use examples of the student's work during each conference to document his or her progress toward reaching specific goals (the student should gradually take more responsibility for documenting progress over the course of the year).

Keep in mind that goals should be specific and moderately difficult (starting with easier goals at the beginning of the year to show students that successfully achieving these goals is possible). All of the goals should be written down to document students' progress throughout the year. These goal sheets could be combined with the monthly curriculum-based assessment or running records/oral reading assessments to put together a fluency portfolio, which could be used in parent–teacher conferences and/or passed along to teachers from year to year to document students' growth over multiple years.

FIGURE 5.4. Procedures to administer monthly *fluency progress monitoring* conferences.

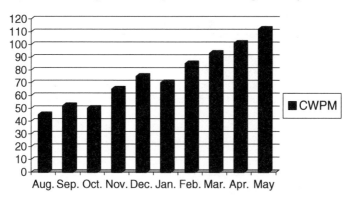

FIGURE 5.5. Example monthly progress chart. *Note.* DIBELS' second-grade fluency benchmark is 90–100 correct words per minute (cwpm).

Finally, almost the entire chapter thus far has focused on students' motivation for reading and what teachers can do to improve that motivation. I would be remiss if I failed to remind you of the influence that your own attitudes and motivations in the classroom have on how your students perceive the activities and tasks that they are required to complete during daily instruction. It is unreasonable to expect our students to get excited about reading and reading instruction if we are not passionate about it ourselves. It is my hope that teachers can use the strategies provided in this chapter as a reference when establishing a motivating classroom atmosphere that not only teaches children how to read, but also teaches them to *enjoy* to read.

CLOSING THOUGHTS

In an era which so much emphasis is being placed on getting students up to "grade level" and preparing them to take high-stakes tests in reading, there is more and more pressure being put on teachers to get through a growing curriculum with seemingly fewer days to do it each year. This mounting pressure makes it easy to overlook the importance of motivating students to enjoy learning and apply what they learn to their daily lives outside of school. I hope I have persuaded you that attention to motivation can make learning more enjoyable, meaningful, and valuable for your students. I also hope I have convinced you that attending to your students' motivational needs is not just mere "fluff" in this era of high-stakes testing, but that it can actually help you accelerate their skill growth in ways that are likely to be reflected in improved test scores after all.

REFERENCES

Ames, C. (1992). Classrooms: Goals, structures, and student motivation. *Journal of Educational Psychology, 84,* 261–271.

Ames, C., & Archer, J. (1988). Achievement goals in the classroom: Students' learning strategies and motivation processes. *Journal of Educational Psychology, 80,* 260–267.

Anderson, R. C., Wilson, P. T., & Fielding, L. G. (1988). Growth in reading and how children spend time outside of school. *Reading Research Quarterly, 23,* 285–303.

Bandura, A. (1986). *Social foundations of thought and action: A social cognitive theory.* Englewood Cliffs, NJ: Prentice-Hall.

Dweck, C., & Leggett, E. (1988). A social-cognitive approach to motivation and personality. *Psychological Review, 95,* 256–273.

Eccles, J. S., Adler, T. F., Futterman, R., Goff, S. B., Kaczala, C. M., Meece, J. L., et al. (1983). Expectancies, values, and academic behaviors. In J. T. Spence (Ed.), *Achievement and achievement motivation* (pp. 75–146). San Francisco: Freeman.

Elliot, A. J. (1999). Approach and avoidance motivation and achievement goals. *Educational Psychologist, 34,* 169–189.

Elliot, E., & Dweck, C. (1988). Goals: An approach to motivation and achievement. *Journal of Personal and Social Psychology, 54,* 5–12.

Good, R. H., Simmons, D., & Smith, S. (1998). Effective academic interventions in the United States: Evaluating and enhancing the acquisition of early reading skills. *School Psychology Review, 27,* 45–56.

Locke, E. A., & Latham, G. P. (1990). *A theory of goal setting and task performance.* Englewood Cliffs, NJ: Prentice-Hall.

Logan, G. D. (1997). Automaticity and reading: Perspectives from the instance theory of automatization. *Reading and Writing Quarterly: Overcoming Learning Difficulties, 13,* 123–146.

Nicholls, J. (1989). *The competitive ethos and democratic education.* Cambridge, MA: Harvard University Press.

O'Flahavan, J., Gambrell, L. B., Guthrie, J., Stahl, S. A., & Alvermann, D. (1992, August). Poll results guide activities of research center. *Reading Today,* p. 12.

Quirk, M. P. (2005). *The development of reading fluency and motivation to read: An examination of the causal relationship.* Unpublished doctoral dissertation, University of Georgia, Athens, GA.

Schunk, D. H. (1991). Self-efficacy and academic motivation. *Educational Psychologist, 26,* 207–231.

Stanovich, K. E. (1986). Matthew effects in reading: Some consequences of individual differences in the acquisition of literacy. *Reading Research Quarterly, 21,* 360–407.

Turner, J. E., Husman, J., & Schallert, D. L. (2002). The importance of students' goals in their emotional experience of academic failure: Investigating the precursors and consequences of shame. *Educational Psychologist, 37,* 79–89.

Weiner, B. (1979). A theory of motivation for some classroom experiences. *Journal of Educational Psychology, 71*, 3–25.

Weiner, B. (1985). An attributional theory of achievement motivation and emotion. *Psychological Review, 92*, 548–573.

Wigfield, A. (1997). Reading motivation: A domain-specific approach to motivation. *Educational Psychologist, 32*, 59–68.

Wigfield, A., & Guthrie, J. T. (1997). Relations of children's motivation for reading to the amount and breadth of their reading. *Journal of Educational Psychology, 89*, 420–432.

CHAPTER 6

Integrating the PHAST and RAVE-O Programs for Struggling Readers

EILEEN A. COHEN, ROSE A. SEVCIK, MARYANNE WOLF,
MAUREEN W. LOVETT, and ROBIN D. MORRIS

THIS CHAPTER DISCUSSES:

- The remedial reading component of the Wide Reading and FORI Programs
- Core learning problems of children who have reading disabilities
- Design and goals of the Georgia State University (GSU) Adapted Fluency Program
- Components of the GSU Adapted Fluency Program
  - Decoding strategies
  - Metacognition
  - Vocabulary
  - Fluency
  - Closure activities
- Teaching cycle

It is a rainy February day in a public school in Atlanta. The school, located in a culturally diverse, urban neighborhood, has many struggling readers. Or, at least that's the way it used to be. From the hallway of one particular second-grade classroom, we can hear the sounds of active learning. Two teachers are working with their remedial reading groups, which consist of four children, in separate corners of the large classroom. The children are so engaged in the lesson that they do not seem distracted by the activities going on in the other group or by the observer who has slipped into the room.

In the first group, each child has a small dry erase board with a word written on it. The teacher and students refer to these words as *challenge words*. When instructed to begin, the children make marks on their board, checking, circling, and underlining parts of the word, and then quickly raise their hand to describe what they have done. One child's explanation sounds like this: "I peeled off *com* at the beginning and *ing* at the end. I see the vowel chunk *a-i-n*. I know the Key Word for that vowel chunk is '*rain*.' So if I know '*rain*,' that must say '*plain*.' Now, I put it back together— *plain—complain—complaining*! I did it—I used Rhyming and Peeling Off and I read the real word—*complaining*" (Lovett, Lacerenza, & Borden, 2000).

The other group is looking at the word *chip* on a dry erase board. The teacher reminds the students that they had thought of so many meanings for this word yesterday, she is sure they are going to be able to cover the whole board with words—and ideas related to the word *chip*. The children can barely stay seated as they stretch their hands up to be called on by the teacher. As the children suggest several meanings for the word *chip*, the teacher records their ideas on the board. She switches colors for each different meaning and for the ideas relating to these meanings. She also draws lines to connect the ideas, creating a web around the word *chip*. The board is almost covered, and the frantic pace has slowed a bit, when one student raises his hand again. With a gleam in his eye, he announces, "I thought of another meaning—the wood chips on the playground"! The teacher praises him for thinking of another different meaning for *chip* and directs the students to refer to their wh-question chart that helps them answer the questions who, what, when, and why. The students think of many words and ideas related to wood chips, and the teacher hastily records their ideas, covering every inch of the dry erase board. The "web" is a colorful mix of words and phrases, and the children beam with pride and excitement (Wolf, Miller, & Donnelly, 2000).

Who are these children? They are participants in the remedial reading component of the Wide Reading and FORI programs. Just 5 short months ago, these children were identified by their teachers as having the lowest reading levels in their classroom. Because of this rating, it was unlikely that they would benefit from either the Wide Reading or the FORI programs without substantial support. In a study of the effectiveness of FORI by Stahl and Heubach (2005), students who were unable to read preprimer

THE GSU ADAPTED FLUENCY PROGRAM

The Georgia State Reading Program was developed as part of a large NICHD (National Institute of Child Health and Human Development) multisite study, involving Robin Morris and Rose Sevcik at Georgia State University, Maureen Lovett at the Hospital for Sick Children, University of Toronto, and Maryanne Wolf at Tufts University in Boston. The GSU Adapted Fluency Program is a combination of the PHAST program developed in Toronto and the RAVE-O program developed in Boston. Combining these programs allowed us to select the most effective strategies and techniques from these highly effective programs to create a multidimensional, research-based program for children at-risk for reading failure.

The authors of this intervention are not alone in this thinking. In fact, the National Reading Panel (2000) concluded that the most effective reading instruction results from a combination of several methods. However, combining methods has both advantages and disadvantages. As we mentioned, one obvious advantage is that the most effective strategies and techniques can be selected from a range of highly successful programs. Combining methodologies also encourages you to be flexible in your use of approaches and techniques, allowing the program to meet a variety of your students' needs. Through this flexibility, you can achieve success with the greatest number of children.

At the same time, there are disadvantages—such as the sheer amount of material you have to cover in the program. Too much information can also cause memory overload for your students and reduce the opportunities for practice and exposure that they need to retain that information. Further, there is limited time in a given day to carry out any remedial program. Because of this constraint, we ended up having to shorten the program more than we might have ideally liked. Nevertheless, when combining the above programs for our remedial approach, we included all the pieces necessary for a complete reading program, but were also scrupulous about including only those skills essential to begin reading.

The Georgia State University Adapted Fluency Program was developed with the support of the National Institute of Child Health and Human Development Grant No. HD30970-05, awarded to Georgia State University, Tufts University, and the Hospital for Sick Children/University of Toronto.

---

texts at the beginning of the second grade made very modest—or no—gains in their reading development. If children are to be able to capitalize on fluency instruction, they need to be armed with the word reading skills upon which fluency instruction is built. In order to achieve this preparation, a pull-out remediation program has been incorporated into our program to meet the needs of these students. We work with small pull-out groups (usually four students to one teacher) that meet on a daily basis. The Georgia State University (GSU) Adapted Fluency Program is the basis of the small-group instruction.

CORE LEARNING PROBLEMS OF CHILDREN WITH READING DISABILITIES

To fully appreciate the program design and the necessity of each element we included in our program, it is important to understand the needs of those students who experience difficulty learning to read. Several common characteristics of these children have emerged through research spanning three decades. You may recognize these issues as ones that are common for the children in your classroom who are having difficulty learning to read.

Phonological Deficits

For more than two decades, researchers have been aware of what they call a *core deficit* in the *phonological,* or sound, components of language for children with reading disabilities. Children with this problem often have difficulty breaking words (or syllables) into sounds. For example, they may be unable to hear that /c/ /a/ /t/ makes up the word *cat* or that *dog* can be broken down into /d/ /o/ /g/. They also have difficulty manipulating these sounds when the sounds are identified for them. For example, they cannot identify rhyming words or mentally take the /c/ off *coat* to get /oat/. Children with reading disabilities often struggle when learning to decode words or when trying to *blend* sounds to produce a spoken word (Lovett, Steinbach, & Frijters, 2000; Foorman, Francis, Fletcher, Schatschneider, & Mehta, 1998; Torgesen, Wagner, & Rashotte, 1997). Weakness in *phonemic awareness,* or the understanding that spoken words are made up of individual sounds (called *phonemes*), adversely impacts the acquisition of early reading skills and makes a child at risk for severe reading difficulties. On the plus side, programs designed to stress phonemic awareness and systematic, explicit phonics training have been shown to be successful in helping most struggling readers "crack the code" of reading. However, these students often remain considerably behind their peers in measures of fluency and reading comprehension (Moats & Foorman, 1997). They also have trouble applying what they do know about word recognition to new situations and seem to learn isolated skills without being able to generalize or transfer that learning. For example, learning words such as *line* and *mark* does little to help these students read *fine* and *dark* (Lovett, Lacerenza, & Borden, 2000). Because of this transfer of learning difficulty, we included elements of the PHAST (Phonological and Strategy Training) program (Lovett, Lacerenza, & Borden, 2000), which combines phonological skill training and *metacognitive* strategy training and in our intervention has been shown to achieve generalization of these skills in struggling readers better than phonological remediation alone.

Visual Naming Speed Deficits

Another characteristic of some children with reading disabilities is a *naming speed deficit*, or a deficit in the ability to rapidly retrieve and name objects presented visually. Children who have naming speed deficits often have reading fluency problems (Wolf, Bally, Morris, 1986; Morris et al., 1998; Schatschneider & Torgesen, 2004). In fact, according to Wolf, "the majority of reading disabled children across all languages and ages tested have naming-speed deficits" (Wolf et al., 2000, p. 375). Further, she believes that this represents a second core deficit among children with *dyslexia*.

Double Deficit

The most profound reading disabilities may belong to yet a third subgroup of children: those who have deficits in *both* phonological knowledge and naming speed. In fact, Wolf and Bowers (1999) believe that in most schools, there is a small group of children who, despite the very best efforts of everyone involved, do not make much progress in learning to read and are sometimes referred to as "treatment resisters" (Blachman, 1994; Torgesen, 2000). We have included features of the RAVE-O (Retrieval Automaticity, Vocabulary Elaboration, and Orthography) program, an experimental reading program with an emphasis on automaticity and fluency, as a means of assisting students with either visual naming speed deficits or this "double deficit" (Bowers & Wolf, 1993; Wolf & Bowers, 1999; Wolf et al., 2000). These features emphasize automatic recognition of common *orthographic patterns*, expanded and flexible *semantic knowledge*, and word-retrieval practice to facilitate rapid word recognition and help children minimize these issues.

Design of the GSU Adapted Fluency Program

To create a successful reading program for students with diverse learning needs, we put much thought into the overall program design and carefully selected the components that went into it. For you to reap the full benefit of this or any reading program, it is important to understand the purpose and goals of each component as well as the relationship between them. According to Adams, "the teacher must understand *why* each activity is included. . . . The teacher must understand how the activities fit together in rationale, dependence and independence, and priority" (1990, p. 423). In order for you to understand the rationale for the GSU Adapted Fluency Program, you should refer to the descriptions of the theoretical principles and instructional practices in Table 6.1. There are also a number of important reading goals that the GSU approach will help your students achieve:

TABLE 6.1. Theoretical Principles and Instructional Practices

- *Combined methodologies*—A variety of methodologies are employed to achieve optimum outcomes with the greatest number of children. Many techniques and approaches are used to teach and reinforce skills and concepts through the visual, auditory, and *kinesthetic* (touch) *modalities.*

- *Direct instruction emphasis*—In direct instruction, both you and your students are actively involved in the entire lesson. Further, whatever time *is* available is utilized for reading instruction. All the tasks are carefully sequenced, moving from the simplest to the most complex. Additionally, all skills that your students are learning are continually reviewed, applied, and reinforced. The activities are designed to solicit correct responses from your students in order to ensure that they do not practice mistakes. Any errors that your children do make are quickly corrected, and they are given the opportunity to practice the correct response immediately. This approach also employs diagnostic teaching in that you are constantly monitoring and assessing your students' progress.

- *Metacognitive component*—Your students are active participants in their learning process, and your instruction makes them aware of what they are doing and why they are doing it. This information allows your students to develop and articulate personal reading goals. They also learn to describe the purpose and application of all the reading strategies that they use.

- *Designed for success*—Initially, you need to model and provide a great deal of guided practice to ensure that your students experience success with each activity. The approach relies on your use of regular positive comments to build success and combat negative feelings about reading. As your students develop confidence in their reading skill, there is a gradual shift in responsibility as your modeling decreases and your students' modeling of the reading skills and strategies increases.

- Developing phonemic awareness—the awareness that language is composed of phonemes, the smallest units of speech, and that these sounds make up a word (e.g., *fish* has three sounds, /f/i/sh/, even though it has four letters, because /sh/ makes up one sound).
- Developing strong phonological skills—learning the connection between letters and their sounds, and the sound blending that is necessary for word decoding.
- Acquiring effective decoding strategies that ensure the transfer of your students' learning to new words.
- Developing automaticity (see Chapter 1) in the recognition of smaller word units (e.g., common letter patterns such as -*ough*, *ir*, *er*, *es*, *ed*, *th*, as well as prefixes, suffixes, and so forth).
- Expanding vocabulary skills to enhance automatic word recognition and reading comprehension.
- Demonstrating increased fluency when reading connected text.
- Achieving a positive change in attitude toward reading and learning by attributing their success to their personal efforts (see Chapter 5).

COMPONENTS OF THE GSU
ADAPTED FLUENCY PROGRAM

Overview

The following components of the GSU program are described in detail:

Decoding strategies
- Preskills
    Phonemic awareness
    Rhyming
- Sounding out
- Rhyming
- Peeling off
- Vowel alert

Metacognition
- Program and personal goals
- Reading umbrella
- Strategy skill review
- Model sentences

Building words
- Word-part cards
- Spell checks
- Magic-*e*
- FATRATS

Vocabulary
- Multiple meanings
- Image cards and props
- Word webs
- Personal sightings/sharings

Speed (automaticity and fluency)
- Quick charts
- Timed readings

Closure activities
- Word building
- Vocabulary

To organize the components of the program for teachers and students, we use a visual aid called the reading umbrella. Figure 6.1 is the teacher version. The student version, which is displayed in the classroom, is shown in Photo 6.1 (p. 109).

Teaching Cycle

How can all of these components fit into one reading program, yet alone one 45-minute block per day? The program is carefully laid out in a 4-day teaching cycle with the fifth day reserved as a consolidation day. You can use this day for reviewing concepts or skills with individual or small groups of children, completing individual assessments and timed readings, and conducting makeup sessions for students who have been absent. If the extra day is not needed, you can simply begin with the next cycle. The teaching cycles are predictable and repetitive, similar to the structure in the FORI and Wide Reading programs. To illustrate the structure of the program, an example of one cycle is included in Figure 6.2.

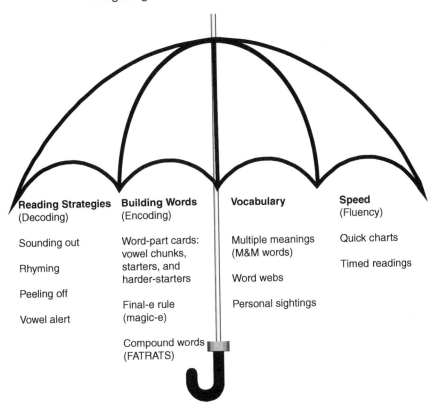

Reading Strategies (Decoding)	Building Words (Encoding)	Vocabulary	Speed (Fluency)
Sounding out	Word-part cards: vowel chunks, starters, and harder-starters	Multiple meanings (M&M words)	Quick charts
Rhyming		Word webs	Timed readings
Peeling off	Final-e rule (magic-e)	Personal sightings	
Vowel alert			
	Compound words (FATRATS)		

FIGURE 6.1. The reading umbrella from the Georgia State University Adapted Fuency Program—Teacher Version.

Decoding Strategies

Preskills

PHONEMIC AWARENESS

As we mentioned earlier, phonemes are the smallest units of speech (e.g., /f/ i/sh/ are the three sounds in *fish*) and a source of difficulty for many struggling readers. Phonemic awareness instruction teaches children to focus on and manipulate these sounds, and provides the foundation for further reading instruction. Although all students benefit from phonemic awareness instruction as part of their early literacy curriculum, most students have mastered these concepts by the end of kindergarten and the beginning of first grade. Unfortunately, it is often the case that the students for whom we have designed this program need additional support in this area. The fol-

	Unit 17	Unit 18	Unit 19	Unit 20
Metacognition	Dialogue for Goals and Purpose Strategy Review #2			
Sounding Out Reading Mastery Fast Cycle (FC)	New sound—/g/ Sound Out: *fun, run, sun, hot*	New sound—/l/ Sound Out: *and, nut, made*	New sound—/w/ Sound Out: *hat, hate, rag*	New sound—/sh/ Sound Out: *sand, hand, land*
Model Sentence		Rhyming	Rhyming	Rhyming
Rhyming	Introduce Key Words: **run, hot**		Key Word Bank Review	
Vocabulary		Image Cards— **run, hot**	Word Web—**run**	
Building Words	Word Part Cards—**un, ot**			Spelling Check
Vowel Alert				
Speed				Quick Chart
Closure	Building Words— Rummy	Vocabulary— Image Card Sorting	Building Words— Magic-e	Vocabulary— Personal Sightings

FIGURE 6.2. An example of one cycle in the GSU Reading Program.

lowing are examples of activities that can help your students develop phonemic awareness. They are meant to be performed aloud.

Phoneme Blending. Draw out the sounds in a word by saying the word very slowly but without pausing between the sounds (e.g., "mmmaaannn") and the child identifies the word. As students become comfortable with this procedure, ask them to say a word slowly by stretching out the sounds and then to say it at its normal rate. This practice prepares students for future lessons in decoding words using sounding out.

Phoneme Segmentation. Say a word aloud and have students break the word into individual sounds by clapping for each sound. A manipulative such as a counter or a small block can also be used to represent each sound. For example, for the word *that*, the child says the word slowly, placing a block down for each sound (three blocks—/th/-/a/ -/t/).

Phoneme Deletion. Ask the students to say what remains when one sound is deleted from a word.

Examples:
Say *win* without the /w/—*in*
Say *cow* without the /c/—*ow*
Say *shape* without the /sh/—*ape*
Say *main* without the /n/—*may*

Phoneme Substitution. Say a word aloud and have the student repeat the word. Then ask him or her to change one sound to another sound and pronounce the new word.

Examples:

lip	change the /l/ to /s/	*sip*
tell	change the /t/ to /s/	*sell*
ram	change the /r/ to /h/	*ham*

RHYMING

The ability to rhyme makes a valuable contribution to your students' acquisition of reading skills (Bryant, MacLean, Bradley, & Crossland, 1990). Children who have solid oral rhyming skills are better prepared to make connections with rhyming words in print (Goswami, 1990). Oral rhyming ability is the foundation for the rhyming strategy, one of the four decoding strategies your children will learn as part of this program. (See the section on rhyming strategy later in the chapter.) To support the development of this skill, you can carry out these activities in this order:

1. Read aloud poems and stories with predictable rhymes and sing rhyming songs to your children (or with them, if they are familiar with a song, poem, or story).

For additional phonemic awareness activities, consider the following research-based programs:

- *Phonemic Awareness in Young Children* by Marilyn Adams, Barbara Foorman, Ingvar Lunberg, and Terri Beeler (1998). This program begins with simple listening and rhyming games and progresses to more advanced sound manipulation exercises such as alliteration and phoneme segmentation.
- *Sounds and Letters for Readers and Spellers* by Jane Fell Greene (1997). This program consists of sequential, cumulative drills to assess and build phonemic awareness.

2. Next, read aloud poems and stories, omitting the rhyming word. Encourage your children to guess the missing word. Here are some recommended rhyming stories:

Julian Jiggs books by Phoebe Gilman (1988)
Digging-est Dog by Al Perkins (1967)
Sam's Lunch Box books by David Pelham (1991)
Hop on Pop (1963), *Green and Eggs and Ham* (1987), and other books by Dr. Seuss

3. Teach your students the rhyming rule: *If two words sound the same at the middle and the end, then they rhyme.* Begin by saying pairs of rhyming words slowly, deliberately emphasizing each sound in the word. Explain to your learners that the words rhyme because they sound the same at the middle and the end. Demonstrate this rule with many pairs of rhyming words. Your children should practice reciting the rule until they have committed it to memory. Finally, present your students with pairs of words that both rhyme and do not rhyme and ask them to state the rule as it applies (or doesn't) to the pairs of words (e.g., the words do not rhyme because they do not sound the same at the middle and the end, or the words do rhyme because they do sound the same at the middle and the end).

4. Continue to practice applying the Rhyming Rule with your students by playing the "Rhyming: Ready, Set, Show" game (see Figure 6.3).

Effective reading instruction for struggling readers must also include a variety of strategies for teaching children how to decode regular words that they have not integrated into their *sight vocabulary*. The GSU reading program includes the following strategies that are designed to help students become effective decoders.

Sounding Out

Sounding out teaches children to sound out unknown words. The program borrows the direct instruction systematic phonics program from SRA Reading Mastery Fast Cycle (Engelmann & Bruner, 1988). Reading Mastery is a highly structured and scripted program that can be controversial. We have heard the program criticized for lacking creativity. However, it is highly effective and an essential part of our program. Shaywitz (2003) recommends "total off-the-shelf comprehensive programs rather than so called eclectic ones that are stitched together by the child's teacher" for instructing students at risk for reading failure. She also highly recommends the Reading Mastery program (pp. 262–263).

With the Reading Mastery program, you teach children the sounds associated with letters and letter combinations and how to blend these

---

Rhyming: Ready, Set, Show

Give the students a 3″ × 3″ piece of poster board and have them draw a happy face on one side and a sad face on the other side. Request that students make the faces large enough to be seen from the back of the room. When all the cards are completed, explain that you will say two words aloud, and then you will say "Ready . . . Set . . . **Show**! If the pair of words rhymes, the students should show the happy face, and if the words do not rhyme, they should show the sad face.

To begin, each student places his or her face cards in front of him or her on the table and you say a pair of words listed below. If any students make an error, say the words slowly, stretching them into their individual sounds (e.g., mmm**aaannn**–fff**aaannn**), emphasizing the middle and final sounds. Also remind the students about the rhyming rule: Words rhyme if they sound the same in the middle and the end.

get–mat	bill–bite	big–rug
cut–nut	mice–nice	rope–hope
stem–hem	bag–rag	cake–lake
talk–walk	care–carry	card–yard
day–pay	night–light	town–down
red–ring	hope–rose	fun–fan
pig–dig	brown–clown	hope–help
slide–hide	zoo–too	hose–nose
play–say	friend–mend	said–so
pine–nine	spell–tell	ride–rest

FIGURE 6.3. Ready, Set, Show game.

sounds together to identify new words. This feature takes place for approximately 20–25 minutes each and every day. This approach teaches difficult sound combinations (e.g., *ou, al, ar*) along with rules for reading long- and short-vowel words such as *tap* and *tape* (final-*e* rule), and *tapping* and *taping* (double consonant rule). In addition to working with individual words, the approach teaches students to apply these skills to connected text, first using simple sentences in student workbooks and then reading stories from the basal reader.

Rhyming Strategy

The next decoding strategy is the rhyming strategy. The rhyming strategy is based on the analogy strategy from the Benchmark Program (Gaskins, Downer, & Gaskins, 1986). When skilled readers encounter an unknown word, they quickly break the word into parts and compare those parts with similar parts in a known word. For example, if you encountered the nonsense word *zight*, you would probably use your familiarity with *-ight* from *light* and *might* to determine its pronunciation. The rhyming strategy teaches students to decode by using such analogies. The approach teaches children to rely on a set of key words to read a word they don't know. For example, your students can use the known key word *nail* to read the unknown word *frail*.

To begin, have your children practice locating vowels in words, then introduce them to the idea of a "vowel chunk," which is defined as "the vowel and the letters that come after it." The vowel chunk is the *phonogram* or *rime* in a word—the part of a single syllable word that one uses to rhyme with words such as (s)*at*, (r)*ock*, or (t)*ip*. Once your students have identified the vowel chunk in a word, ask them to spell out the letters that make up the chunk. For example, for the word *spin*, your children would say "*i*"-"*n*." After much practice locating the vowel and identifying the vowel chunk in words, you should guide your students to the discovery that "words with the same vowel chunk usually rhyme."

You can select the most common and useful phonograms for beginning readers by choosing from Wylie and Durrell's (1970) list of 37 phonograms, which allows you to derive nearly 500 primary-grade words. The list can be found in Figure 6.4.

We cross-referenced Wylie and Durrell's list with the RAVE-O and PHAST programs to create a final list of 56 vowel chunks. The key words and their phonograms are listed in Figure 6.5. One rhyming key word is selected for each vowel chunk; for example, *cap* is the word for *-ap*.

To introduce new key words for the rhyming strategy, we use the *mnemonic* of a cardboard door and large key to help children remember the strategy. The following excerpt from a typical class shows how you would introduce the new key word *kick* and demonstrates the use of the mnemonic devices:

> Margaret Ellis displays a large cardboard door and a large key for her students. The new key word *kick* is displayed on a card attached to a large cardboard key. The first letter, *k*, is black and the vowel chunk, *-ick*, is color-coded blue. The children sound out the word using the sounding out strategy. The teacher replies, "*Yes, kick; I like to* **kick** *my soccer ball.*"

-ack, -ail, -ain, -ake, -ale, -ame, -an, -ank, -ap, -ash, -at, -ate,
-aw, -ay, -eat, -ell, -est, -ice, -ick, -ide, -ight, -ill, -in, -ine, -ing,
-ink, -ip, -it, -ock, -oke, -op, -ore, -ot, -uck, -ub, -ump, -unk

---

FIGURE 6.4. Wylie and Durrell's (1970) list of the most common phonograms.

Lots of hands shoot up as the students anticipate the teacher's next question. "The vowel chunk is -*ick*!" offers a student. Hands shoot up again as the students clamor for the opportunity to offer words that rhyme with the new key word, "*Sick*"!, "*Rick*"!, "*Lick*"!, "*Quick*"!

Then Ms. Ellis directs their attention to the rhyming door, and with a flourish, she uses the key to open the door and reveal a list of words that can be "unlocked" using the new key word. The words are color coded to emphasize the vowel chunk. The children are called on, in turn, to demonstrate the rhyming strategy on these words using the following dialogue: "If I know *kick*, then I know *quick*."

This procedure continues until the students have read all the words on the list. The teacher reminds the students that the key words are important because they can unlock and open the door to all the words with the same vowel chunk, and she guides the students to add the new key word to the key word bank. The key words we use can be found in Figure 6.5.

The following list shows how your key word bank should look when you're finished. For color coding of spelling patterns, use the following scheme: a = red; e = green; i = blue; o = orange; u = purple.

a	e	i	o	u
cab	ear	kick	boat	tub
pack	heat	kid	rock	duck
mad	bed	ride	rod	bug
tag	see	pig	dog	jump
nail	well	bill	joke	run
rain	pen	him	cold	lunch
cake	end	pin	top	junk
walk	nest	sink	more	nut
ram	set	ship	hot	
game		fish		
man		sit		
band				
bank				
cap				
care				
cash				
cat				
ate				
play				

FIGURE 6.5. Key word bank: A display with the key words sorted and alphabetized according to the vowel chunk. Adapted from Gaskins, Downer, and Gaskins (1986). Copyright 1986 by Benchmark School. Adapted by permission.

To introduce a new strategy, write a sentence on the board and model the application of the strategy on the sentence. You should also model the dialogue that is specific to that strategy and will eventually be used by the children when they are applying the strategy. To show the students how to apply the rhyming strategy to read unknown words, write the following sentence on the board (or choose an appropriate sentence based on the reading level of your students):

The *van* has a *flat*.

Say: "I am going to show you how I can use the rhyming strategy to read words that I don't know." Point to the first underlined word and say, "I see a vowel chunk I recognize. It is *-a-n* [spell it out], and I know a key word for that vowel chunk. It is *man*. I know that words with the same vowel chunks usually rhyme, so this word must rhyme with *man*. If I know *man*, this word must be *van*." Repeat the procedure for the word *flat* using the key word *cat*. Conclude by reading the sentence aloud: "Listen while I read the sentence aloud to see if the words *van* and *flat* make sense. 'The van has a flat.' Yes, that makes sense; the van must have a flat tire. I did it! I used rhyming to read the words *van* and *flat*"! The self-congratulatory remarks are important to encourage your students to attribute successful word reading to knowledge and use of the decoding strategies.

Peeling Off

Peeling off is a strategy for decoding multisyllabic words containing *affixes*. The approach is designed to help your students identify common prefixes (referred to as "beginnings") and suffixes (referred to as "endings"). The terms *beginnings* and *endings* are substituted for the words *prefix* and *suffix* to encourage the students to attend to affixes. Children learn to remove these affixes from the root word in order to help them with their decoding. They read or decode the root word using sounding out, the rhyming strategy, and peeling off and then reassemble the parts to read the whole word. By practicing peeling off, they learn to quickly recognize affixes in real words, which allows them to segment multisyllabic words quickly. This strategy is very satisfying to the students because they are able to break longer words into manageable parts by removing prefixes and suffixes, enabling them—often for the first time—to read "big" words.

New affixes are introduced at a rate of one per week. Write each of the affixes on paper "leaves" (green leaves for prefixes and orange leaves for suffixes), and, as you introduce each affix, post it on a large tree poster. The tree is the mnemonic device to remind students that affixes, like leaves on a tree, can be removed. The tree also serves as a means of displaying the affixes for regular review. Here is an example of how one of our teachers, Richard Levine, follows the program to introduce a new affix:

> Mr. Levine presents the new affix written on a green leaf. "Is this a beginning or an ending?"
>
> Students quickly respond, "Ending!"
>
> "Yes, and it is pronounced *-tion*." A student models the application of the strategy on the word *prevention* written on a long card. She says, "I see *pre-* at the beginning, so I can peel off *pre-*. I see *-tion* at the end, so I can peel off *-tion*." She folds the card back to "peel off" the affixes, until finally only the root word remains. "Now I'll read the root—I see the vowel chunk, *-e -n*. I know a key word for that vowel chunk—it's *pen*. If I know *pen*, then this must say *-ven*. Now I'll put the word back together: *-ven*, *preven-*, *prevention*. PREVENTION— that's a real word. I did it! I used peeling off and rhyming to read the word *prevention*.

You can then lead the group in a review of all affixes, pointing to one at a time and pronouncing each in unison. Reading the individual affixes aloud repeatedly develops automatic recognition of them and enhances students' ability to apply the peeling off strategy. Students are then given worksheets with lists of multisyllabic challenge words. They quickly locate and circle the affixes and are then called upon to model the peeling off strategy on these words. The teacher models the process first:

> "When I come to a word I don't know, first I look at the beginning and the end to see if there is anything that I can peel off. I see [name the affix] at the beginning [or the end], I peel off [name the affix], and the root is [name the root]. I put the word back together. The whole word is [name the word]."

Vowel Alert

The vowel alert strategy introduces children to the idea that vowels are tricky because they have more than one sound. It also teaches them how to deal with this ambiguity by using context to verify decoding accuracy. For this strategy, first introduce your students to the variable pronunciations of single vowels. Then move on to vowel combinations and teach them cue words for the following vowel combinations:

Double-Trouble Twins
ow—as in *cow* or *glow*
oo—as in *zoo* or *look*
ea—as in *sea* or *head*

Extend the application of this strategy with the following consonant letters, which are shown to have variable sounds as well:

C & G Alert
c—as in *cat* or *city*
g—as in *girl* and *giraffe*

In order for your students to practice the vowel alert strategy, give them sets of word cards that they can sort and arrange in columns under the corresponding cue word (e.g., *now* and *how* would go under *cow*, whereas *crow* and *mow* would go under *glow*). After your children have finished sorting these cards, they should read through the columns aloud for you to check for accuracy.

Here is an example of how one of our teachers, Sharon Hamilton, teaches children to use the vowel alert strategy:

> Ms. Hamilton writes the sentence *A brook ran through the park* on the board. She points to the underlined word and says "Look at this word. I am going to show you how I use the vowel alert to read this word. I see the double trouble twin -*oo* and know I have to be flexible." She points to a Stop Sign hanging on the wall to remind children to stop and use the vowel alert strategy. "I'll stop and try both sounds. First I'll try *oo* as in *zoo*—*brook*. Is that a real word?"
>
> "No!" mumble several students.
>
> "So I will try the other sound—*oo* as in *look*—*brook*. That is a real word. Let's see if that word makes sense in the sentence. *A brook ran through the park.* A brook is a small stream or creek, and a stream or brook could run through a park. I did it! I used vowel alert to read the word *brook*."

Metacognition

The metacognitive lessons involve your students directly in the learning process and facilitate their ability to effectively and efficiently select and apply decoding strategies to unfamiliar words. They also learn how to monitor and evaluate their strategy use and to note explicitly their active role in successfully decoding the word. The students learn that their success is related to their own thinking skills and knowledge of word decoding strategies. Without this emphasis, struggling readers are unlikely to develop metacognitive strategies on their own and are likely to attribute whatever successes they do experience to *good luck* rather than their own ability.

As each decoding strategy, reading skill, and activity is introduced to your students, post it in the classroom under a "reading umbrella," our means of organizing the program for the students. The reading umbrella

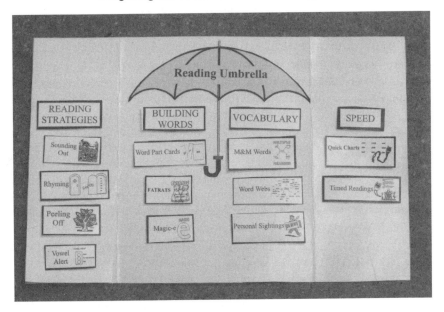

PHOTO 6.1. The Reading Umbrella from the Georgia State University Adapted Fluency Program—Student Version.

(see Photo 6.1) is a visual aid that helps your children see and understand all the skills they are learning as well as how these skills connect to help them become better readers. Your students should be able to describe how they can use each of the reading skills, and it is important that you review these skills with them frequently. It is also useful to refer to the reading umbrella during these reviews.

The metacognitive lessons are staggered in presentation over the course of the school year. The following overview illustrates the sequence of introduction:

- Discussion of program and personal goals.
- Reading umbrella—a visual aid to help your children understand the organization of the program.
- Reading strategy review lessons—developing common terms to describe various aspects of decoding strategies your students will be using, such as:
    Sounding out—when describing the sounding-out strategy, the students learn to say, "I say the sounds the letters make, blend the sounds, and then say the word."
- Model sentence decoding—the teacher and eventually individual students demonstrate decoding strategies on sentences.

Discussion of Program and Personal Goals

From day 1, your students will be involved in listening to and stating the program goals. By having regular discussions about why reading is important, you help your students discover and verbalize their own personal reading goals. To enhance these discussions, you and your students can create a collage with pictures of people reading (library catalogues are good sources) and various samples of reading material. Among the many things you can include are maps, signs (traffic and billboard), recipes, instructions (e.g., games, toys, auto maintenance, medications) catalogs, music, books, magazines, newspapers, and so on. This collage serves as a visual aid that helps your students keep in mind the many reasons for learning to read and allowing even your most struggling reader to participate in the discussions you are holding regarding reading.

Reading Strategy Review Lessons

In these lessons your students practice specific verbal guidelines that describe the decoding strategies they are learning. They begin by reviewing the steps in the first strategy, sounding out, and then they progress to the other strategies, as they are taught. These memorized verbal guidelines lead to efficient strategy use as the students learn to "talk themselves through" the selection and application of the decoding strategies. Examples of the guidelines learned for each strategy follow.

- *Sounding-out strategy*—"I say the sounds the letters make, blend the sounds and say the word."
- *Rhyming strategy*—"I see a vowel chunk I recognize. The vowel chunk is -i-c-k [spell out the letters], the key word is *kick*. If I know *kick*, this word must be *brick*." The students also define key words as words they already know that help them read words they don't know.
- *Peeling off strategy*—"When I come to a long word I don't know, first I look at the beginning and the end to see if there is anything that I can peel off. I peel off the beginnings and the endings, read the root word, and put the word back together to read the whole word."
- *Vowel alert*—"Vowels are tricky because they have more than one sound. If I read a word and it doesn't sound like a real word, I stop and try both sounds for the vowel. For the double-trouble twin *ow*, first I'll try *ow* as in *cow*, and then *ow* as in *glow*."

Model Sentences

As mentioned previously, a sentence is used in the introduction of each strategy. The sentence is written on a white board, and using the guideline specific to each strategy, you demonstrate decoding words in the sentence. This modeling of strategy application on sentences continues throughout the program. The words in the sentence get increasingly difficult and frequently require more than one strategy for decoding. Sentences are used so that you can demonstrate the use of context to check decoding accuracy. Initially, you demonstrate only successful strategy application and include affirmations attributing successful decoding to your own effort. Eventually, unsuccessful attempts at decoding should also be modeled, demonstrating how you select another strategy until you are able to decode the word. Gradually, your students are given the responsibility of demonstrating the decoding strategies on the model sentences.

Building Words

Up to this point in the program, the reading skills and strategies primarily involve decoding—or breaking a word into its components. The building words lessons and activities involve *encoding*—or putting the letters and letter patterns together to form words. Building words activities are designed to reinforce and extend concepts presented in the program. To help your children recognize common phonological patterns in words, they use hands-on practice with manipulatives, called word-part cards, that include common rime patterns (e.g., -at, -ine, -op) and beginning consonant letters. The students "build words" by adding consonant letter cards to the rime pattern (vowel chunk) cards. A more challenging activity, called spell checks (described below), requires children to write words with the newly learned rime patterns. Further, the idea of compound words and rules such as the long-vowel final -e are taught.

Word-Part Cards

To provide hands-on practice with newly learned rimes, word-part cards are used with your group each time a new key word is introduced. This activity begins by providing your students with packs of starter and vowel chunk cards and a building words record sheet that lists the rimes on which the students are currently working at the top in columns. Students form words by combining the "starters" (beginning consonants) or "harder starters" (consonant digraphs and blends) and the vowel chunks (rimes; e.g., adding *s* to *at* would give them *sat*). They then record their words under the appropriate rime ("vowel chunk") on their building words record sheet. The starters and harder starters can be displayed in the classroom for the students to refer to when they are building words. Figure 6.6 is an example of the building words record sheet. We used *The Reading Teacher's Book of Lists* (Fry, Kress, & Fountoukidis, 2000) to create the starter and harder starter poster in Figure 6.7.

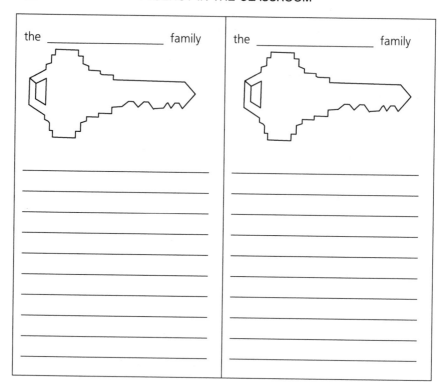

FIGURE 6.6. Building words record sheet.

Spell Checks

To ensure consolidation of the vowel chunks (the rimes) and the initial consonant sounds (including consonant digraphs and blends) and to develop effective encoding (spelling) skills, the students are given weekly spell checks on the key words and rhyming words for the week.

To begin the assessment, call out a key word; your students record the word in the drawing of the key at the top of one column of the spell-check sheet (see Figure 6.8). Initially, the children can copy the key word; however, they should eventually be able to spell the key word independently. It is essential that the key word be spelled correctly before proceeding. Repeat the procedure with the second key word, with the students writing that key word in the key at the top of the second column. Once the key words are written correctly, you call out rhyming words that use the same rime patterns as the key words, and your students write the word in the column

Starters and Harder Starters

Starters
b
c
d
f
g
h
j
k
l
m
n
p
qu
r
s
t
v
w
y
z
ch
sh
th
wh

Harder Starters

r	l	s	t	3 letter
dr	fl	st	tw	thr
fr	sl	sc		str
tr	cl	sn		scr
br	pl	sw		spr
cr	bl	sm		shr
gr	gl	sp		spl
pr		sk		squ
				sch
				chr

Silent	Exceptions
wr	ph
kn	

FIGURE 6.7. Harder Starter Poster

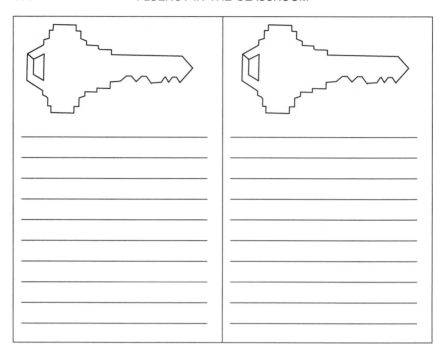

FIGURE 6.8. Spell-check sheet.

under the correct key word. In addition to spelling the word correctly, your students must be sure to record the word in the correct column. Finally, each child should have the opportunity to check his or her paper, and any corrections should be made immediately.

Magic-e

To give your students practice with final-*e* words, prepare large cards with the letters of the alphabet. Select several of your students to stand up and hold letter cards to make a word (e.g., *c-a-n*) that you or they can read aloud. Another of your students is selected to be the magic-*e*. He or she will wave a magic wand over the vowel within the word and then step to the end of the word holding the letter card *e*. The student holding the vowel calls out his or her name (in this case, "*-a*"), and the whole group says the new word *cane*. Words that can be used for magic-*e* activities are listed in Figure 6.9.

hop	hope	at	ate
fin	fine	hid	hide
rat	rate	fad	fade
slop	slope	cut	cute
pin	pine	shin	shine
tap	tape	can	cane
mat	mate	cap	cape
pan	pane	bid	bide
fat	fate	slat	slate
man	mane	dim	dime
hat	hate	nap	nape
kit	kite	gap	gape
slid	slide	rid	ride
bit	bite	rod	rode

FIGURE 6.9. Magic-*e* word list.

FATRATS

To provide practice in recognizing and decoding compound words, the children are taught to look for whole words within a word. They know that two whole words are *FATRAT words* or compound words. They also practice putting single-syllable words together to form compound words. Games and activities to extend the concept are included in the Closure Activities section.

Vocabulary

Vocabulary is critical to all reading. It is hard to envision being a competent reader without an adequate vocabulary for comprehending what is read. Vocabulary is also important for word recognition, which goes faster when the reader knows or can easily retrieve the meaning of the words being read (Schwanenflugel & Noyes, 1996). A limited vocabulary can hamper the reading progress. We wish to avoid the following problem:

Anita, a second-grade student, sounded out the word *fin* beautifully. However, because she did not know what the word meant, she stared blankly at the teacher and shrugged her shoulders, being unsure that she had produced a real word.

The vocabulary activities of this program serve several reading purposes, but their primary goal is to support automatic word recognition. These vocabulary activities can help your students develop an interest in words and foster an appreciation of the richness of the language. This vocabulary work expands your student's knowledge of words through exploration and discovery of meanings and the uses of words in a variety of interesting formats. The key words selected for other aspects of the program are also used here because they were selected for both their orthographic patterns and their rich and various meanings.

Image Cards and Props

After the key words are introduced and their orthographic characteristics are studied, the focus shifts to the meanings of these words. Remind your students that one word can have many meanings and ask them to think about the meanings for the featured word. As your students offer definitions for the word, you should present them with an "image card" or a picture representing the meaning they offer. If there is no image card to match a definition they think of, they can quickly illustrate that definition. Props can also be used to expand and enrich the discussions of the multiple meanings of a word. For example, for the word *jam*, you could provide toy cars to illustrate a traffic jam. Similarly, for the word *sand*, wood and sand paper may be provided for sanding. In addition to enhancing the discussions of the multiple meanings of the word, such props also seem to aid some children in the recall and retrieval of words. For example:

> Jason, a student with severe word-retrieval difficulties, had particular difficulties reading words with the *-ick* rime pattern. He was unable to read the word *stick* until the teacher brought a hockey stick to the classroom. When Jason encountered a word with the *-ick* rime pattern afterward, he would mouth the word *hockey* as an aid to recalling the *-ick* pronunciation.

Word Webs

Another weekly vocabulary activity is the creation of a word web. The web allows your children to recall the many meanings for one of the vocabulary words studied that week. Through the web, your students can expand their understanding of the many meanings of the word and see the interconnectedness of words. A "who, what, when, where" chart is used to stimulate the students' reflections about the many words, phrases, and ideas related to the word. You should record your students' ideas in a web that is formed around the word. Each time a new meaning or use for the word is mentioned, you should change to a different color marker as a means of keeping the concepts distinct. Through your collaborative effort, your students and you will be able to cover the entire board with a colorful mix of words, phrases, and expressions related to one small word. This accomplishment is often a source of pride for the students, who like to compare their webs to those completed by other reading groups.

Personal Sightings/Sharing

Children enjoy being asked to be word detectives—that is, people who are always watching and listening for the words they are learning. As a conclusion to the week's vocabulary work, your students are given the opportunity to share any experiences they have had with the key words. Some good prompt questions include the following:

Has anyone "eaten" one of these words? (e.g., *cake, chips, nuts, dates*)
Did anyone "do" any of the words? (e.g., *play* a game, *stand* in a line, *walk* a dog)
Did you "use" any of the words? (e.g., write with a *pen*, fix something with a *pin*)
Did you "feel" any of the words? (e.g., feel *well*, feel *mad*, feel *hot* or *cold*)

Speed: Automaticity and Fluency

The goal of all these program components is to help your students develop automatic decoding and word recognition. According to Lyon (1999), reading words accurately is a necessary skill in learning to read, but the speed at which this occurs is a critical factor in ensuring comprehension (see also Chapter 1). If word reading is laborious, little cognitive resources remain for understanding what is read. Therefore, being able to read quickly is a primary goal of this reading program. The focus of these activities is on both reading individual words and drawing on all reading skills and strategies to read connected texts.

To monitor the development of automaticity and fluency, timed readings of both single words and short stories should occur regularly. Each week, your children should be timed as they read through the key words on a chart called the quick chart. For the quick chart, the words are displayed in rows (left to right) and each student reads through the words as quickly as possible. After everyone has had a turn, they get a second chance to beat their original score. For connected text, you should copy texts that you are reading on a single page, marking every 20th word so that you can quickly determine the number of words children read in 1 minute. Your students then practice reading with a partner as they wait for their turn to be timed by the teacher. This practice helps prepare them for the partner reading they will be doing as part of the FORI program.

Closure Activities

Materials from the program are used in game-like activities at the end of each lesson. In addition to reinforcing and consolidating basic reading skills, these activities can motivate students to work hard to earn game time. The word building and vocabulary units lend themselves especially well to the closure activities.

Building Words Closure Activities

WORD-PART GAME

In this activity you give each of your students their own sets of word-part cards with both starters and vowel chunks (rimes). Your students then try to see how many words they can make within a given amount of time, recording them in their notebooks as they go along. Once time has been called, have your students read the words they made to one another. Each real word (even if they are duplicates) should earn one point. Your students can try to beat their totals from the previous sessions.

WORD-PART RUMMY

For this activity, shuffle the starter cards and place them on the table. Give each of your students two or three vowel chunk cards. Each student draws a starter card and tries to make a word using this starter card and one of the vowel chunk cards in his or her hand. Each word should then be placed on the desk in front of the student who formed it. Turns should continue until all the cards are used to form words or no other words can be made from the available cards.

MAGIC-*E* FLASHCARDS

You can make flashcards with words that follow the long -*e* rule and their short-vowel counterparts (e.g., *kit* and *kite;* refer to Figure 6.9). Have your students read the words as a group using the traditional flashcard format. They can follow-up this activity by sorting the flashcards into two piles: words with and without the magic-*e*.

MAGIC-*E* MEMORY GAME

This game makes use of matched pairs of magic-*e* flashcards. Lay the cards face down in neat rows on the table. As students each takes a turn, they turn over two cards and read the words. If they have a magic-*e* pair, they keep the pair and get one more turn; if the pair doesn't match, the next child gets to go.

HARDER STARTER HUNT

In this activity, your students are given a list of words that contain consonant blends, which we call *harder starters*. Their job is to go through these words and underline or highlight these blends or harder starters. You can also give them old newspapers or magazines in which they can also hunt for harder starters.

FATRATS BINGO

Blank bingo sheets (nine squares—three columns by three rows) can quickly be turned into a compound word bingo game. Have the students name compound words that you record on a white board (about 15 words). Give each student a blank bingo sheet along with bingo chips (e.g., small pieces of construction paper, pennies). Tell your students to select nine of the compound words from the list on the white board and write them randomly on their bingo sheets. To play, you should call out one word at a time in random order (pulling the words out of the bag creates the atmosphere of a game of chance). When one of your students marks three words in a row (diagonally, vertically, or horizontally), he or she calls out "BINGO!"

FATRAT MATCHING

Compound words are written on index cards and then cut up into two separate words, making two piles: words that make up the front half of the compound word and words that make up the second half of the compound words. Mix up each of the piles, taking care not to mix the front halves and the back halves of the words together. It then becomes your students' job to reassemble the cards in order to reform the compound words.

MYSTERY WORD

This game, similar to Hangman, is designed to provide your students with practice spelling words they have already learned as part of the program.

To play the game, you think of a word, note the number of letters in the word, and write one blank space for each letter on the board (e.g., ___ ___ ___ ___ ___). You should also draw 10 X's on the board. Each student takes a turn guessing a letter. When a correct answer (letter) is given, you write that letter in the appropriate blank space. When an incorrect answer is given, you should record that letter on the board and erase one of the X's. The game is over when the letters are all filled in, all of the X's are erased, or when one of your students correctly guesses the word.

Vocabulary Closure Activities

IMAGE CARD SORTING

In this activity, the students work in pairs, sorting the image cards by placing them in pocket charts next to the corresponding word card. In our experience, great discussions can ensue as students defend their choice of image cards for the definition.

DEFINITION DUEL

In this activity, your class is divided into two teams. A word card is drawn from a pile and displayed in clear view. The teams then compete to see which group can think of the most definitions for a word.

"WHAT'S MISSING?" GAME

To play, place props on the table for your students to study. Your students are told to close their eyes while one object is removed and then challenged to guess the missing item.

IMAGE CARD CHARADES

As with traditional charades, students act out a definition, but in this case, an image card is selected as the basis for the charade. Students are called on to guess the word.

CLOSING THOUGHTS

The result of combining these research-based reading programs is very powerful. Our research on this program has indicated that teachers feel empowered by it and that children make substantial, accelerated progress. When compared to a control group of children who were developing reading skills at the expected rate, the at-risk readers appeared to be on the same trajectory of reading skill acquisition by the end of the intervention. At the beginning of the intervention, the at-risk readers were reading sight words but had no decoding skills. In the control group, the students recognized more words by sight and were using phonetic decoding skills to read unknown words. By the end of the intervention, the control group students were reading grade-level text fluently. The students in the remediation groups had expanded their sight vocabularies, and more importantly, had developed the ability to use decoding skills to read unknown words. Expanding their sight vocabulary and developing word-reading skills meant that they now had the skills they needed to participate in and benefit from, the fluency instruction in the FORI and Wide Reading programs taking place in their classrooms. The students seemed to be aware and proud of their accomplishments in reading. For the first time, many children see themselves as readers. As one our students put it, after leaping up and making contact for the first time with the top of the door jam, "Wow, I can read faster *and* jump higher!"

ACKNOWLEDGMENTS

The Georgia State University Adapted Fluency Program was developed with the support of National Institute of Child Health and Human Development Grant No. HD30970-05 awarded to Georgia State University, Tufts University, and the Hospital for Sick Children/University of Toronto. We gratefully acknowledge the efforts of all the teachers who contributed to and taught the GSU Fluency Program. Very special thanks to the GSU team, Mary Bucklen, Victoria Burke, Kim Imbrecht, Heather Lubeck, Judi Mahoney, Cashawn Myers, Priscilla Noble, Nioyonu Olutosin, and Sonja Ross for their invaluable contributions to the program. Thank you also to Justin Wise for his support and technical help in the writing of this chapter.

REFERENCES

Adams, M. J. (1990). *Beginning to read: Thinking and learning about print*. Cambridge, MA: MIT Press.

Adams, M. J., Foorman, B. R., Lundberg, I., & Beeler, T. (1998). *Phonemic awareness in young children*. Baltimore: Brookes.

Blachman, B. A. (1994). What we have learned from longitudinal studies of phonological processing and reading, and some unanswered questions: A response to Torgesen, Wagner, and Roshotte. *Journal of Learning Disabilities, 27*(5), 287–291.

Bowers, P. G., & Wolf, M. (1993). Theoretical links among naming speed, precise timing mechanisms and orthographic skill in dyslexia. *Reading and Writing: An Interdisciplinary Journal, 5*, 69–85.

Bryant, P. E., MacLean, M., Bradley, L. L., & Crossland, J. (1990). Rhyme and alliteration, phoneme detection and learning to read. *Developmental Psychology, 26*(3), 429–438.

Engelmann, S., & Bruner, E. C. (1988). *Reading Mastery I/II Fast Cycle: Teacher's guide*. Chicago: Science Research Associates.

Foorman, B. R., Francis, D. J., Fletcher, J. M., Schatschneider, C., & Mehta, P. (1998). The role of instruction in learning to read: Preventing reading failure in at-risk children. *Journal of Educational Psychology, 90*(1), 37–55.

Fry, E., Kress, J., & Fountoukidis, D. (2000). *The reading teacher's book of lists*. Englewood Cliffs, NJ: Prentice-Hall.

Gaskins, I. W., Downer, M. A., & Gaskins, R. W. (1986). *Introduction to the Benchmark School word identification/vocabulary development program*. Media, PA: Benchmark School.

Gilman, P. (1988). *Julian Jiggs*. New York: Scholastic.

Goswami, U. (1990). A special link between rhyming skill and the use of orthographic analogies by beginning readers. *Journal of Child Psychology and Psychiatry and Allied Disciplines, 31*(2), 301–311.

Greene, J. F. (1997). *Sounds and letters for readers and spellers: Phonemic awareness drills for teachers and speech–language pathologists*. Longmont, CO: Sopris West Educational Services.

Lovett, M. W., Lacerenza, L., & Borden, S. L. (2000). Putting struggling readers on the PHAST track: A program to integrate phonological and strategy-based remedial reading instruction and maximize outcomes. *Journal of Learning Disabilities, 33*(5), 458–476.

Lovett, M. W., Steinbach, K. A., & Frijters, J. A. (2000). Remediating the core deficits of developmental reading disability: A double-deficit perspective. *Journal of Learning Disabilities, 33*(4), 334–358.

Lyon, G. R. (1999). Statement of Dr. G. Reid Lyon, April 28, 1998. In *Reading research anthology: The why? of reading instruction* (pp. 13–23). Novato, CA: Arena Press.

Moats, L. C., & Foorman, B. R. (1997). Introduction to special issue of SSR: Components of effective reading instruction. *Scientific Studies of Reading, 1*, 187–189.

National Reading Panel. (2000). *An evidence-based assessment of scientific research literature on reading and its implications for reading instruction*. Washington, DC: National Institute of Child Health and Human Development.

Pelham, D. (1991). *Sam's lunch box*. New York: Penguin Group, Dutton Children's Books.

Perkins, A. (1967). *The digging-est dog*. New York: Random House.

Schatschneider, C., & Torgesen, J. K. (2004). Using our current understanding of dyslexia to support early identification and intervention. *Journal of Child Neurology, 19*(10), 759–765.

Schwanenflugel, P. J., & Noyes, C. R. (1996). Context availability and the development of word reading skill. *Journal of Literacy Research, 28*, 35–54.

Dr. Seuss (Geisel, T. S.). (1963). *Hop on Pop*. New York: Random House.

Dr. Seuss (Geisel, T. S.). (1987). *Green eggs and ham*. New York: Random House.

Shaywitz, S. E. (2003). *Overcoming dyslexia*. New York: Vintage Books.

Stahl, S. A., & Heubach, K. M. (2005). Fluency-Oriented Reading Instruction. *Journal of Literacy Research, 37*(1), 25–60.

Torgesen, J. K. (2000). Individual differences in response to early interventions in reading: The lingering problem of treatment resisters. *Learning Disabilities Research and Practice, 15*(1), 55–64.

Torgesen, J. K., Wagner, R. K., & Rashotte, C. A. (1997). Prevention and remediation of severe reading disabilities: Keeping the end in mind. *Scientific Studies of Reading, 1*(3), 217–235.

Wolf, M., Bally, H., & Morris, R. (1986). Automaticity, retrieval processes, and reading: A longitudinal study in average and impaired readers. *Child Development, 57*(4), 988–1000.

Wolf, M., & Bowers, P. G. (1999). The double deficit hypothesis for the developmental dyslexias. *Journal of Educational Psychology, 91*(3), 415–438.

Wolf, M., Miller, L., & Donnelly, K. (2000). Retrieval, automaticity, vocabulary elaboration, orthography (RAVE-O): A comprehensive, fluency based reading intervention program. *Journal of Learning Disabilities, 33*(4), 375–386.

Wylie, R., & Durrell, D. (1970). Teaching vowels through phonograms. *Elementary English, 47*, 787–791.

CHAPTER 7

The Family and Fluency
Developing the Home–School Connection

LESLEY MANDEL MORROW

THIS CHAPTER DESCRIBES:

- A family literacy program designed to help second- and third-grade children to become more fluent readers.
- How the Family Fluency Program was developed from the school fluency program with second-grade children.
- The sessions provided for families at school to learn about the program.
- What the family involvement at home entailed.
- The results of the Family Fluency Program.

Mrs. Martinez walked into the all-purpose room at school for the meeting about families and the fluency program in which she was going to be involved. She had her three grandchildren with her: one was a second grader in the fluency program, one was a third grader, and the last was a preschooler. She was raising these children. She seemed hesitant about joining us, so I went to greet her. We found a place for her to sit next to a parent she knew. One of our assistants brought Mrs. Martinez and her grandchildren juice and cookies along with the materials we would use in the program that evening. A few minutes later John, age 13, brought his sister Kim, who was in the second-grade fluency program, to school. He dropped her in the room and went outside to play basketball on the school playground until she was ready to go home. Kim felt quite alone surrounded by children with their caregivers. Although John was playing basketball, he frequently glanced our way, as if he wanted come into the school program but also felt hesitant since he wasn't an adult. We asked John if he wanted to join us, and he said okay. Kim seemed very pleased, and we got them some juice and cookies, the materials for the program, and a place to sit. However, many came to the meeting feeling quite comfortable in the school environment and began socializing as they settled in. There were many stories to tell about many of the families that came to the meeting. The group was extremely diverse, representing multiple cultural backgrounds. We were delighted to have what we felt was a full house for our meeting.

Throughout this book, my colleagues have discussed the importance of fluency development. When children are fluent, they read automatically and with prosody. When children read automatically, they are able to decode words quickly and accurately (Kuhn & Stahl, 2003). When they read with prosody, they use the appropriate pitch, pace, and expression (Schreiber, 1987, 1991). Fluent reading acts as an aid to comprehension. According to the National Reading Panel (2000) report, fluency is a predictor of reading success. It has been found that although reading fluency is a major goal in the reading instruction, teachers are not as familiar as they should be with fluency strategies (Rasinski, 2003). It is often assumed that automatic decoding abilities will inevitably lead to fluency. Because this is not necessarily the case, students need to participate in fluency-oriented instruction (Allington, 1983; Reutzel, 1996). *Families* can be an important part of that instruction.

The success of a literacy program depends, to a certain extent, on the literacy environment at home. As such, it is crucial for the school to involve families as an integral part of the literacy instruction. What do we mean by *family*? A family is any group of people who is involved in the direct care of children. This can be grandparents, as in the case of Mrs. Martinez, or it can be an older sibling who is mature and responsible enough to care for younger siblings, such as John. It can also be aunts and uncles, stepparents, older cousins, foster parents, close family friends and other unrelated adults who live with the children (sometimes called *fictive kin*) who have the trust of the children's parents for caregiving. These extended family networks are very common among African American, Native American, and Hispanic American families in this country and operate in an "It takes a village . . . " manner to raise children (Wilson, 1989).

Schools need to let family members know how they can help at home by supporting the school program. Family members need to be informed about the school literacy program. Family members need to come to school events that teach them about involvement at home whenever they can. Similarly, family members need to spend time in their children's classrooms as often as possible to help them better understand the literacy programs. Family members should also be involved in the assessment of their child's progress.

Family literacy programs have successfully promoted interactions between children and their family members with many types of literacy events. *Home–school programs* need to be easy to use and include activities done in school and practiced at home. Further, whatever materials are sent home should first be introduced to the children in school. The content should be nonthreatening, and the activities should be fun (Morrow & Young, 1997; Morrow, Scoblionko, & Shafer, 1995).

The *Family Fluency Program* introduced family members whose children were in either the Wide Reading or Fluency-Oriented Reading Instruction (FORI) fluency programs at school to strategies that they could carry out at home and that would engage their children in fluency development experiences. Further, in the study that we carried out to evaluate the effectiveness of the program, we found that the family members who participated in the workshop sessions we provided about fluency . . .

- Engaged in fluency activities at home.
- Had a heightened awareness about the importance of fluency training in their child's literacy development.
- Increased the level of literacy involvement at home with their children.

THE FAMILY FLUENCY PROGRAM: THE HOME–SCHOOL MEETINGS

The Family Fluency Program was an important part of the overall intervention and was conducted in both the Wide Reading and the FORI schools reported in Chapter 2. There were two major components for the family members. First, we sent home the texts that the students were reading each week in order for the children to read the selections repeatedly with their family. Families were asked to fill out slips to document whether they read with their child. Second, we offered three evening sessions for family members: one in October, one in February and one in April. We wanted to heighten awareness about the importance of fluency, to describe the school program, and to discuss the activities that family members could do at home in order to enhance their children's fluency.

When working with family members, the greatest fear is that no one will show up at school meetings such as this one. We had such an experience at one school in the program. Teachers had expected 100 people based on the stated intention of the children's families, so we ordered pizza and drinks for that number. Instead, 15 family members showed up for the meeting. Needless to say, there was lots of pizza for teachers in the teachers' lounge the next day and the day following! Getting family members to attend these meetings can be a difficult and frustrating task. But there are ways to increase your chances of high attendance at all three family sessions.

The First Family Workshop

We sent home several notes and made phone calls to ensure that there would be good attendance at the first workshop. Teachers helped us by reminding the children to remind their family members before, and on the day of, the meeting. Members of the project team also visited the classrooms that were participating in the project on the day of the meetings to urge the children to remind their families. Children were invited to the meeting to participate and show off the fluency practices to their family members. This element helped to increase family attendance. Because the children were invited to participate, they encouraged their family members to take them. Another advantage to inviting the children is that it encourages families to attend because they enjoy seeing their children engaged in school activities.

The first training session for families was successful, with 35 family members and about 50 children. The family members brought their second graders as well as some older and younger siblings. After some refreshments, the children went to another room with teachers to supervise them. We worked with the family members first to describe the school program. We reviewed the purpose of the program and discussed the strategies being used in school. We then described the home program and demonstrated the strategies with a short selection similar to stories children were reading in school. We talked about building background for the story before it is read, and how to connect the story to the lives of the children. If the story was about weather, for example, we suggested a discussion about the type of weather their child liked the most and why, such as rainy days, sunny days, cold days, warm days. Family members were encouraged to enter into the conversation as well. We demonstrated echo reading, choral reading, and partner reading. Using the same story, we engaged the family members in a discussion prior to reading. Then we asked the family members to try the fluency strategies with us.

We echo-read the short story, with one of us reading one line and then the caregivers repeating that line. We used appropriate expression and pace and discussed how this process demonstrates fluent reading to the children. Then we choral-read the same story, which meant that we all read the story together. However, the lead teacher set the tone for the pace and expression to model for the group. We even demonstrated what is called *antiphonal choral reading*. In this type of choral reading the group is divided into two or three subgroups that are assigned different parts to choral-read at different times. Finally, in pairs, we engaged the caregivers in partner reading. During this activity, we asked the partners to look at the pictures and discuss what they already knew about the story from having read it. Then the partners decided who would read first; the first reader read one page and the next reader read the next page until the story was done. At the end of the story, the partners talked about the parts they liked best and how the story connected to their lives.

We also discussed the importance of oral reading and how it provides a sense of community. We talk about how oral reading by teachers and family members gives them the opportunity to provide a good model for reading as the children follow along. We also discussed why we were repeating the same story so often. The repetition is one way to help with decoding, learning new vocabulary, understanding the text, and using the correct pace and expression. We also provided family members with a handout in English and Spanish that explained these strategies (see Figure 7.1).

We invited the children back into the room, and this time we worked with another very short story. The story, *The Little Red Hen,* was one we thought everyone might know well and would be easy and fun to work with. We talked about the story by looking at the pictures before we began and discussed how it was about a hen who wanted help baking some bread, but none of her friends would participate. We asked if anyone had had that experience. Juan told us how his brother wouldn't help clean up their room and how he had to do it all by himself. One mom talked about how her kids loved to eat her dinner but not help clean it up. Then we read the story to the group as a whole. Next, the family members and children echo-read along with us. After echo reading, we all choral-read the story, and finally each family member and child partner read the story together, using the framework for partner reading described earlier.

We reminded the family members that they were to read the stories that were sent home and record that they did so on the forms we included. We encouraged the family members to use the fluency strategies with their children many times during the week. When we finished with the workshop, we spent some time socializing with the participants while enjoying refreshments. Because not all of the intervention families came to the session, we sent home the packet of materials that had been provided with their children the following day. We also made follow-up phone calls to see that they received the packets and to review the materials with them.

The Second Family Workshop

A second meeting was held midyear to discuss what families and children were doing at home. We asked the children and their family members what

---

Reading Activities to Do with the Books Your Child Brings Home from School

- *Echo Reading:* You read one line and the child reads the same line after you. Increase the number of lines you read at one time as the child's reading improves. To be sure that the child is looking at the words, ask him/her to follow the print with a finger. Try to echo-read at least one story each week.

- *Choral Reading:* You and your child read the same text aloud, together. Choral reading should be done at least twice a week.

- *Partner Reading*: You and your child take turns reading. Start by reading one sentence and asking the child to read the next sentence. As the child's fluency improves, you read a page and he/she reads a page. Partner-read about once a week.

- *Repeated Reading:* Read the same book or story more than once in the same week.

- *Remember:* Whenever you read with your child, remember to use as much expression as you can so your reading sounds like speaking and the story comes alive.

Actividades de Lectura Que Puede Hacer Cuando Su Hijo Trae Libros de la Escuela a Su Hogar

- *Lecturas eco:* Usted lee una linea y su niño lee la misma linea después que usted haya completado la línea. Aumente el número de líneas que usted lee a medida que su hijo mejore su lectura. Para estar seguro de que su niño observa las palabras mientras que lee, pregúntale que señale con su dedo a medida que lee cada palabra de la oración. Intente la estrategia de eco por 10 menos una vez en semana.

- *Lecturas en coro:* Usted y su niño pueden leer del libro simultáneamente en voz alta. Esta estrategia se debe llevar a cabo por lo menos dos veces en semana.

- *Lecturas en parejas:* Usted y su niño deben alternar turnos al leer. Primero, usted lee una oración y luego pídale a su niño que lea la próxima oración. A medida que la fluidez de su niño progresa, usted puede leer una página y luego su niño, la otra página. Esta estrategia de lectura en parejas se debe hacer una vez en semana.

- *Lecturas repetidas:* Lea el mismo libro o el mismo cuento más de una vez durante la misma semana.

- *Recuerde:* Cuando le lee a su niño, recuerde que debe emplear muchas expresiones enfáticas para que el cuento suene como si estuviera hablándole al niño y el cuento tenga vida.

FIGURE 7.1. Caregiver handout for the Family Fluency Program.

they liked best about the program: repeating the readings, the discussions, echo reading, choral reading, or partner reading? It seemed as if echo and partner reading were more popular than choral. We asked for their thoughts and feelings about the activities, and we answered questions they raised. We had made a video of the children in their classrooms participating in echo, choral, and partner reading, which was thoroughly enjoyed by the family members, teachers, and children. We reviewed the strategies for the new families that had not been to the first meeting. We had 30 family members attending and 40 children. Most were from the first meeting, but five were new. Nine family members who had been to the first meeting did not attend the second.

We provided the families and children with a fluency evaluation form so that they were aware of what constituted good fluent reading. We played a tape of excellent fluent reading, good reading, and reading that was just okay. We evaluated the tape recording that was excellent first and called this *Wow* reading; it flowed smoothly and at a good pace, all words were decoded properly, and the reader's use of expression demonstrated understanding of the text. We listened to *Good* reading and discussed the characteristics. *Good* reading was done at a pace that was slow but not choppy, and words were pronounced properly with enough expression to show some understanding. Finally, we listened to and evaluated what we called *Okay* reading. This reading was word by word, slow, choppy, lacking expression, and some words were read incorrectly. We suggested that, in addition to doing the fluency activities with their children, the families could also tape-record them and evaluate the recordings together. They could also make a second tape at a later date, which they could listen to and compare to the earlier tape. This comparison would allow them to discuss the children's progress. We told the families that we would send tape recorders home with their children if they needed them. Family members and children also received a handout to help them remember the evaluation system (see Figure 7.2). We again ended the meeting with refreshments.

Evaluate Fluency

Here are some guidelines for evaluating fluency:

1. Tape-record your child reading a passage about once a month.
2. Play the previous month's recording to listen for improvement.
3. Evaluate the reading as *Okay*, *Good*, or *Wow*.

- *Okay:* Reading is word-by-word, slow, and choppy, with some words missed and not enough expression to show an understaning of the text.
- *Good:* The pace of the reading is slow but not choppy. Most words are pronounced properly and with enough expression to show some understanding of the text.
- *Wow:* Reading flows smoothly at a good pace. All words are decoded properly and expression demonstrates an understanding of what is being read.

FIGURE 7.2. Handout providing guidelines for caregivers on evaluating fluency.

PHOTO 7.1. Two brothers partner-read at home following a family fluency meeting.

The Third Family Meeting

At the third meeting we invited the children and the caregivers again. At this meeting one group of children performed an echo reading, another group performed a choral reading, and two children illustrated a partner reading they had practiced with their teachers. As mentioned earlier, having the children participate in the family meetings proved to be an effective way to motivate the family members to come and, consequently, to participate at home. As always, we served refreshments. At the end of the meeting caregivers received a VIP certificate, meaning *Very Involved Participants.*

THE POSITIVE RESULTS
OF THE FAMILY FLUENCY PROGRAM

To find out if the family involvement program was successful, we asked teachers to report how involved they felt the family members of children in their classrooms were in terms of reading to, or with, their children at home. Teachers used a scale that we provided in order to rank caregivers from 1 to 5, with 5 indicating a lot of home involvement and 1 indicating very little home involvement. The average for teachers ranking the extent of home involvement for families who participated in the program was 3, whereas the average for teachers ranking caregiver involvement in the classrooms that didn't participate was 2.

We also used a survey to determine family involvement. The survey was sent home with the children and asked family members how often they were able to help children with homework, how often they were able to read to or with, their children, and how they felt they could help their children become fluent readers. We received 35 surveys back from the family members who participated in the program, and 28 from family members who did not take part. The information received from the family members was promising. Sixty-nine percent of those who completed surveys and were involved in the program said that they helped their child with homework five times a week compared to 45% in the group who did not participate. Forty-six percent of the family members in the program reported reading to, or with, their children five times a week. In the group that did not participate, that number was only 9%.

Families were asked how they helped their children become more fluent readers. Those in the program group showed an understanding of how to help children become fluent readers. They listed the strategies they were taught at the home–school sessions and used the vocabulary involved in fluency instruction. For example, family members talked about the importance of practicing reading with their child by repeating the same story over and over, echo reading, choral reading, and reading with a partner. They talked about helping their children read at the right pace—not too fast and not too slow—and to read with expression. They also mentioned sounding out words and being patient with their children. All of these activities develop fluency.

The family members in the group that did not have the program used some of the fluency terms but in a less consistent manner and had more of a variety of responses. Their responses were good responses but not for the matter of developing fluency. This group of families mentioned that phonics was the most important element to create fluent readers, reading to your child, reading more difficult books with their child, helping with writing and spelling, playing reading games, and encouraging children to read on their own.

FAMILY, CHILD, AND TEACHER INTERVIEWS

We also interviewed children, family members, and teachers by asking them questions related to the Family Fluency Program. We received a range of answers and created a list of comments based upon them. If an answer occurred more than once, it was not repeated on our collective list.

Children who participated in the Wide Reading and FORI groups were asked, "How do you feel about the Family Fluency Program?" Here are examples of the answers given:

"I don't feel alone when I'm reading."
"I will know how to help my children when I grow up. I will read the same stories over again with them, we will partner-read, and we will choral-read. When they really need help, we will echo-read."

"It is nice to read with someone else. Sometimes you think they don't care about your schoolwork or you, but when they read with you, you know they do."

Examples of answers given by family members in response to the same question include these:

"It was fun to work with my child."
"My child looked forward to working with me."
"I learned how to help my child with reading that I didn't know about before."
"I learned some things about reading from my child, since my English isn't so good."
"I just thought you helped children sound out words; now I know reading the same story over and over is important."
"I never knew about reading together—they called it choral reading."
"I never knew about partner reading and taking turns."
"The activities were easy to do and didn't take much time."
"I could see an improvement in my child's reading as a result of the repeated reading that we did."

Among the responses given to the same question by teachers in the program groups are the following:

"Families in the program read with their children more than families I have had in the past."
"Family members definitely learned the techniques to enhance fluency—they recorded on their forms echo reading, choral reading, and partner reading."
"Families recognized and mentioned the improvement they saw in their children's reading by repeating stories."
"I saw improvement in many of my struggling readers as a result of the repeated readings at home. Their decoding and comprehension of repeated stories improved. It also raised their self-esteem."

CLOSING THOUGHTS

Working with families is always a challenge, but it is also very important and can be very rewarding. We feel that the Family Fluency Program was successful for several reasons. The activities are easy to understand and initiate; they take a short time to carry out and bring about results quickly. Family members could see a change in how children read as they repeated stories. They talked about improved pace and expression. They talked about less choppy reading and better understanding. The program heightened their awareness about the use of oral reading strategies to help their children, and the activities enhanced family involvement in literacy activities at home. We do not know if the Family Fluency Program enhanced the fluency of our students because the number of students involved were not large and the surveys were done anonymously, making it impossible to link child outcomes to particular families. But the information we collected and reported on showed some promising and positive outcomes as a result of the Family Fluency Program. Family literacy programs have been successful at promoting parent–child interaction with many types of literacy events. Home–school programs need to be easy to use. Materials sent home must be introduced to children in school first. The content should be nonthreatening and the activities need to be fun. We believe that the Family Fluency Program has all of these characteristics!

REFERENCES

Allington, R. L. (1983). Fluency: The neglected reading goal. *The ReadingTeacher, 36,* 556–561.

Kuhn, M. R., & Stahl, S. (2003). Fluency: A review of developmental and remedial practices. *Journal of Educational Psychology, 95,* 3–21,

Morrow, L. M., Scoblionco, J., & Shafer, D. (1995). The family reading and writing appreciation program In L. M. Morrow (Ed.), *Family literacy connections in schools and communities* (pp. 70–86). Newark, DE: International Reading Association.

Morrow, L. M., & Young, J. (1997). A family literacy program connecting school and home: Effects on attitude, motivation, and literacy achievement. *Journal of Educational Psychology, 89,* 736–742

National Reading Panel. (2000). *Teaching children to read: An evidence-based assessment of the scientific research literature on reading and its implications for reading instruction. Reports of the subgroups.* Bethesda, MD: National Institutes of Health. Available at *www.nichd.nih.gov/publications/nrp/.*

Rasinski, T. V. (2003). *The fluent reader: Oral reading strategies for building word recognition, fluency, and comprehension.* New York: Scholastic Professional Books.

Reutzel, D. R. (1996). Developing at-risk readers' oral reading fluency. In L. R. Putnam (Ed.), *How to become a better reading teacher* (pp. 241–254). Englewood Cliffs, NJ: Merrill.

Schreiber, P. A. (1987). Prosody and structure in children's syntactic processing. In R. Horowitz & S. J. Samuels (Eds.), *Comprehending oral and written language* (pp. 243–270). New York: Academic Press.

Schreiber, P. A. (1991). Understanding prosody's role in reading acquisition. *Theory Into Practice, 30,* 158–164.

Wilson, M. N. (1989). Child development in the context of the black extended family. *American Psychologist, 44,* 380–385.

CHAPTER 8

Assessing Reading Fluency

JUSTIN MILLER and CAROLYN A. GROFF

THIS CHAPTER INCLUDES:

- A discussion of the use of curriculum-based assessment of oral reading fluency.
- A description of common types of curriculum-based assessments.
- Guidelines for choosing a "good" standardized test.
- A discussion of how to use the normative information provided by standardized tests of fluency.
- A description of some popular standardized assessments of oral reading fluency.

As teachers, it is natural to believe that what and how we teach are the important elements of our instruction and that assessment is somehow secondary to that. Perhaps you might even believe that the time spent on assessment directly conflicts with the goal of actually teaching. You may ask yourselves, "With all of this emphasis on assessment these days, when do I get the chance to teach what I need to teach?"

We are sympathetic. However, we would like to convince you that good assessments are, in fact, integral to your teaching. Without them, you would not have any tangible evidence as to whether your children are making the progress that you think they should. You would not know whether some children have particular needs that are not being met. Further, you might be uncertain as to whether a particular teaching practice is working for all—or only some small portion—of your students. In short, without good assessment, your teaching might not really be as effective as you think it is.

There are several reasons why you might want to assess your students' reading fluency. First, knowledge of your students' reading ability will allow you to determine the appropriate difficulty level of text for each student; this will help at-risk readers develop their fluency, and it may allow you to determine that fluency instruction is necessary only for a select group of students. Second, when carried out on a regular basis, fluency assessments can help you chart the growth of both individual students and your entire classrooms. Regular assessment would also allow you to determine whether your current instructional strategies are effective or whether you may need to try other approaches. Finally, assessing oral reading fluency may also be necessary to evaluate more severe reading difficulties and to determine the appropriateness of special education placement. The goal for this chapter is help you become familiar with a range of fluency assessments, both curriculum-based and standardized, that are commonly used in schools and other educational settings.

CURRICULUM-BASED ASSESSMENT OF ORAL READING FLUENCY

Curriculum-based assessments are those designed for the purposes of instructional planning and monitoring student progress through course content (Burns, MacQuarrie, & Campbell, 1999). These assessments are typically administered by teachers and are used for classroom purposes only. Curriculum-based assessments are usually informally administered, which allows some latitude in how the directions are presented, whether or not a student is helped or prompted, and the manner in which a response is determined to be correct. And while they cannot be used for special education classification or the provision of other special services, they can inform your decision-making processes within the classroom. Fortunately, we have several curriculum-based assessments of fluency at our disposal (McKenna & Stahl, 2003; Rasinski, 2003).

Reading Rate

Reading rate is a very important indicator of reading fluency (Schwanenflugel et al., 2006). The first curriculum-based assessment measures children's reading rate by calculating the number of correct words per minute (cwpm) on the reading of a short passage. In order to implement this assessment, identify a target passage and make a copy of it. You also need a stopwatch or a watch with a second hand. Ask your student to read out loud for 1 minute while you mark every miscue on your own copy of the text. Also mark the final word that the student read on your copy. Finally, count the number of words in the passage up to that point. This assessment is quite easy to score using the following formula:

$$cwpm = \text{total number of words read in 1 minute} - \text{the total number of miscues}$$

You should use selections from your classroom reading series or a trade book that you are using as part of your literacy curriculum to assess your students. Resources provided by Fountas and Pinnell (1996) or Gunning (1998) can help you determine the level of these texts. Using a classroom text allows you the opportunity to observe your students' progress on your classroom material.

Figure 8.1 shows such an assessment carried out with Jemarcus, who was asked to read a grade-level text created by Miller and Schwanen-

circle
Frog and [*pause*] Toad were happy, [*long pause*] playful, [*long pause*] curious animal

friends. [*pitch decline, pause*] One afternoon, [*pause*] near a pond in the [*pause*] forest, [*pause*]
tail
Frog and Toad played [*pause*] together. [*pause*] They sp- sp- spotted a trail in the [*pause*]

distance. [*pause*]

"Where do you think it goes?" [*pitch decline, pause*] asked Frog. [*pause*]

"Let's find out," [*pause*] said Toad.

They started down the path. [*pitch decline, pause*] They came upon a cabin with a pretty, [*pause*]
grand
colorful, [*pause*] tidy garden hidden behind a fence. [*pause*]

"Do you see anyone inside?" [pitch rise, pause] asked Toad. [*pause*]

"No, I can't see [*pause*] anything," [*pause*] said Frog.

The house looked empty. [*pause*]
stop
"Should we go over there and look?" asked Frog.

"I don't know. How did we get in?" asked Toad.

Frog and Toad wanted to look around. Nobody was home, but it seemed that someone

might live there.

FIGURE 8.1. An example of a third grader, Jemarcus, carrying out an oral reading of an excerpt from a passage by Miller and Schwanenflugel (2006).

flugel (2006) in a study of oral reading fluency and prosody during the fall of his third-grade year. Jemarcus read a total of 81 words in 1 minute and made three miscues. Thus, by subtracting the number of miscues from the total number of words read, Jemarcus's cwpm score would be calculated as 78.

Once a student's cwpm score has been determined, it is important to look at grade-level norms to assess how he or she is developing relative to other students. These norms indicate, in a general way, where a student's development should fall in terms of both grade levels and across three time points within a school year (usually fall, winter, and spring). The norms presented in Table 8.1 are from those reported by Hasbrouck and Tindal (2006). Looking at Jemarcus's score of 78, we can see that he is about average for third graders at this time of year.

We would like to make two additional points about using cwpm as a measure of reading rate. First, norms such as these represent an average reading rate in each quartile. This means that if some of your students' rates fall more than 10 words below the 50th percentile average, they are likely in need of additional fluency instruction or further assessment. For Jemarcus, we would conclude that he is performing as expected for his age. Second, these norms reflect the fact that, over the summer, most students lose some ground in their reading rate from the previous spring. This explains why the averages provided for the spring of an academic year are generally higher than the norms for the fall of the following academic year. Thus, Jemarcus may have actually read at a higher cwpm rate during the spring of his second-grade year; however, with effective literacy instruction, he should make up this lost ground and achieve additional progress over the course of third grade.

TABLE 8.1. Fluency Norms for the Early Elementary Grades

| Grade | Percentile | cwpm | | |
		Fall	Winter	Spring
1	75	N/A	47	82
	50	N/A	23	53
	25	N/A	12	28
2	75	79	100	117
	50	51	72	89
	25	25	42	61
3	75	99	120	137
	50	71	92	107
	25	44	62	78

Note. Data from Hasbrouck and Tindal (2006).

Ratings of Fluency and Expression

According to Kuhn and Stahl (2003), many studies measuring fluency focus on rate and accuracy, perhaps because they are the most easily recognizable elements of fluent reading. Less easy to recognize, yet integral to sounding like a fluent reader, are the prosodic elements such as pausing and phrasing. *Prosodic reading* involves the use of expression and appropriate phrasing (see Chapter 1). Because the use of appropriate expression is, to some degree, subjective, it is more difficult to measure than rate and accuracy. Fortunately, several scales used to measure fluent reading have been designed to include prosodic, expressive reading elements. Scales such as the National Assessment of Educational Progress (NAEP) Oral Reading Fluency Scale (White, 1995) and the Multidimensional Fluency Scale (Zutell & Rasinski, 1991) can be used to evaluate students' fluency from a more global perspective. Like reading rate, the NAEP scale or the Zutell and Rasinski scale can be used with the texts designed to be part of your literacy curricula (e.g., basals, literature anthologies, or guided reading books), trade books, or texts designed for reading evaluation (e.g., materials designed specifically for assessment).

The NAEP Oral Reading Fluency Scale, which is the most widely used of such scales, focuses on the following key elements of oral reading: (1) the grouping of words, or the phrasing and pauses, along with the perceived rise and fall in pitch; (2) the reader's ability to adhere to the syntax and sentence structure of the text, which is critical to smooth oral delivery and indicates the reader's awareness of the ideas being expressed; and (3) the general expressiveness of the oral reading. Such a scale provides a broad generalization of a child's oral reading fluency and can be used rather easily with anything that the child reads aloud. Passage readings are assigned a rating from 1 to 4, with the skill designations presented in Table 8.2.

Many first graders read word by word and therefore would be assigned to NAEP level 1. By the beginning of second grade, they have typically progressed to two-word phrases, yet still lack appropriate expression (NAEP level 2). As students in second grade become more competent, their reading takes on more appropriate phrasing and expression, so that by the end of second grade and into third grade, they are often incorporating prosodic elements (NAEP level 3 or even 4). As with students who are making inadequate progress in terms of reading rate, those whose expressive oral reading remains at level 1 and 2 beyond the beginning of second grade are likely in need of supplemental fluency instruction. It is important to remember that the gradual incorporation of prosodic elements is more likely to occur when you regularly model fluent reading and encourage your students to practice such reading on a regular basis.

We can use the NAEP scale in relation to our earlier example of Jemarcus and note several features that can be used to assign an appropri-

TABLE 8.2. NAEP Oral Reading Fluency Scale

Level 4

Reads primarily in larger, meaningful phrase groups. Although some regressions, repetitions, and deviations from text may be present, they do not appear to detract from the overall structure of the story. Preservation of the author's syntax is consistent. Some or most of the story is read with expressive interpretation.

Level 3

Reads primarily in three- or four-word phrase groups. Some smaller groupings may be present. However, most phrasing seems appropriate and preserves the syntax of the author. Little or no expressive interpretation is present.

Level 2

Reads primarily in two-word phrases with some three- or four-word groupings. Some word-by-word reading may be present. Word groupings may seem awkward and unrelated to the larger context of sentence or passage.

Level 1

Reads primarily word by word. Occasionally two- or three-word phrases may occur, but these are infrequent, and/or they do not preserve meaningful syntax.

ate rating. First, we can see that his reading is characterized by frequent and inappropriate pausing, especially when he encounters difficult words. In addition, Jemarcus used all the punctuation (including all commas) as an indication that he should pause; however, fluent readers do not necessarily pause at all commas, such as those in lists. On the positive side, Jemarcus does read in predominantly three- or four-word groupings, although there are some smaller groupings as well. Similarly, Jamarcus is able to integrate some expression into his reading, but inconsistently. For example, he raises his voice at every question mark, even though it is only mandatory for yes–no questions. Quite clearly, Jemarcus is still learning to integrate what he is being taught about punctuation (e.g., pause at commas, raise your voice when you come to a question mark) in a rather robotic fashion. As he becomes an increasingly competent reader, his use of these elements will become more natural and less mechanical. Taking the pattern of word groupings, pausing, and pitch changes presented here into account, we assigned Jemarcus's oral reading a NAEP oral fluency rating of 3.

More complex systems for rating oral reading fluency include the Multidimensional Fluency Scale. Rasinski (2004), one of the authors of the scale, suggests, that separate ratings on three distinct aspects of reading (phrasing, smoothness, and pace), in addition to expression and volume, provide a more detailed evaluation of fluency than single-dimension scales and is better able to capture the strengths and weaknesses of individual readers. Each of the three dimensions consists of a 4-point rating system (see Table 8.3).

TABLE 8.3. Multidimensional Fluency Scale

Expression and volume

1. Reads words as if simply to get them out. Little sense of trying to make text sound like natural language. Tends to read in quiet voice.
2. Begins to use voice to make text sound like natural language in some areas of the text but not in others. Focus remains largely on pronouncing the words. Still reads in a quiet voice.
3. Makes text sound like natural language through the better part of the passage. Occasionally slips into expressionless reading. Voice volume is generally appropriate throughout the text.
4. Reads with good expression and enthusiasm throughout the text. Varies expression and volume to match his or her interpretation of the passage.

Phrasing

1. Monotonic with little sense of phrase boundaries; frequent word-by-word reading.
2. Frequent two- and three-word phrases, giving the impression of choppy reading; improper stress and intonation that fails to mark ends of sentences and clauses.
3. Mixture of run-ons, midsentence pauses for breath, and possibly some choppiness; reasonable stress/intonation.
4. Generally well-phrased, mostly in clause and sentence units, with adequate attention to expression.

Smoothness

1. Frequent extended pauses, hesitations, false starts, sound-outs, repetitions, and/or multiple attempts.
2. Several "rough spots" in text where extended pauses, hesitations, etc., are more frequent and disruptive.
3. Occasional breaks in smoothness caused by difficulties with specific words and/or structures.
4. Generally smooth reading with some breaks, but word and structure difficulties are resolved quickly, usually through self-correction.

Pace (during sections of minimal disruptions)

1. Slow and laborious.
2. Moderately slow.
3. Uneven mixture of fast and slow reading.
4. Consistently conversational.

Note. Based on Zutell and Rasinski (1991).

Going back to our example, Jemarcus showed reasonable stress and intonation but had a number of midsentence pauses for breath and decoding issues. So, for *expression and volume,* we would assign him a 3. For the *phrasing* subscale we would also assign him a 3. Similarly, because disruptions in *smoothness* cause by difficulties with specific words characterized most of the breaks in Jemarcus's fluent reading, we would assign him a 3. Finally, because of the mixture of pausing and slow reading, we would rate his reading on the *pace* subscale a 3.

In carrying out curriculum-based assessment, we recommend combining the NAEP or Multidimensional Fluency Scale with measurements of reading rate. For example, if we look across Jemarcus's scores, we can see that, in every respect, he appears to be showing typical development as a fluent oral reader. He falls in the average range in cwpm norms, and his ratings on both global fluency scales are what we would expect for his grade level. Given this, you could decide that, for Jemarcus, the fluency instruction that you are providing for the class as a whole is probably sufficient. Further, there does not seem to be a need for additional testing because there are no concerns regarding potential fluency difficulties.

Other Guidelines for Curriculum-Based Assessment

When assessing your students' oral reading fluency using curriculum-based assessments, we think a few guidelines should be considered. First, your students need to be evaluated using a text passage that they have not had the opportunity to practice reading. This stipulation differs from standard practice during literacy instruction where, with few exceptions, your students would have practiced reading their text before being called on to read aloud.

Second, grade-level texts should be used as at least one part of your fluency assessment. If you know that your students will not be able to even approach fluent reading of such passages, then you should begin your assessments with a more appropriate text and progress through more challenging material until they can no longer read fluently. Using this process, you can gain a sense of what material your students can handle independently, how much support they will need to succeed with your mandated texts, and whether there is a need for fluency-oriented reading instruction.

Finally, it is recommended that you make tape recordings of your students' oral reading fluency to ensure the accuracy of your evaluations. Because each reading lasts only 1 minute, your entire class's oral reading should fit onto a single cassette tape. Recordings enable you to render more accurate evaluations for two reasons. First, you can mark any miscues you might have missed during the actual assessment, and second, you can relisten for phrasing and expression to obtain the most appropriate NAEP or Multidimensional Fluency Scale rating. Because prosodic elements can be difficult to assess, listening to the recordings can help you confirm that you are recognizing these elements correctly.

An additional but equally important goal for curriculum-based fluency assessment is to determine each student's independent, instructional, and frustrational reading levels. To do this, you must understand how the percentage of correct words per passage is thought to correspond with each level. If a student's correct words per passage is 95% or higher, then the passage is considered to be at his or her independent level; this designation means that the child should be able to read the passage without much assistance from an adult. A score of 90–94% indicates that the passage is at his or her instructional level—which means that this is text would be appropriate to use during instruction or some other minimally scaffolded setting where a more knowledgeable adult or student can assist in the reading of the text. A score below 90% suggests that the passage is at the student's frustration level (Clay, 2002). We would not expect the child to read this text in the classroom or certainly by him- or herself without some exceptional scaffolding techniques such as those described in Chapters 2, 3, and 4. It is also important to realize that although some students read with great accuracy, their reading is extremely slow, and they incorporate few expressive elements. In this case, students should read instructional-level texts with support to develop their speed and prosody.

TRACKING READING GROWTH AND EXAMINING INSTRUCTION EFFECTS

Curriculum-based assessments can be used to track students' oral reading growth. For example, if you wished to examine the effects of repeated readings on a child's reading fluency, you could track his or her progress by recording the reading rate and number of miscues over the course of several repeated readings. Or you might have students keep track of their own progress. By noting their improvements, students may become more motivated to read and may be less frustrated when they make errors (see Chapter 6).

Such assessments might also be used to determine whether a particular passage is too difficult to use for fluency practice. According to Reutzel (2003), the bulk of a student's growth occurs between three and five repetitions. If a student does not show signs of progress by the fifth repetition, it is an indication that the text being used for the measure is too difficult, and a new text on the student's instructional level should be used (see Dowhower, 1989, or Rasinski, 2003, for a full description of the repeated readings procedure).

Of course, the issue of using curriculum-based assessments to examine the effects and benefits of instruction is more general than its use for evaluating repeated readings. The technique can be used to examine the effectiveness of other practices on the development of student fluency as well.

STANDARDIZED ASSESSMENT OF READING FLUENCY

Standardized measures of fluency differ in a number of important ways from curriculum-based measures. *Standardized assessments* have clearly specified administration and scoring procedures. Unlike curriculum-based assessments, where measurements can be taken on performances using a variety of texts or materials and where there is flexibility in the presentation of directions and scoring, standardized tools are carefully constructed and prohibit any deviations from their prescribed protocol. Yet, it is precisely this characteristic of standardized measures—the assurance that each child was assessed in exactly the same way and that his or her responses were scored similarly—that permits us to make a variety of meaningful comparisons. Thus, standardized assessments are most often used for diagnostic purposes regarding special education classification or the provision of special services within the school. Further, these measures are generally administered by school psychologists, psychometricians, reading specialists, or others who have certification and special training in standardized assessment. Table 8.4 lists the distinctions between curriculum-based and standardized assessment.

In the next section, we describe essential terms and concepts that you need to know about standardized fluency assessment. We also introduce specific examples of standardized fluency measures that are commonly used by reading specialists, psychologists, and other education professionals.

What Constitutes a "Good Test" of Reading Fluency?

Whenever a test of reading fluency (or, for that matter, any test) is administered, it is important that you have some assurance that the test meets basic standards of quality. First, you would want to be sure that children obtain similar scores if they are tested again under similar condi-

TABLE 8.4. Differences between Curriculum-Based and Standardized Assessment

Feature	Curriculum-based	Standardized
	Test type	
Purpose	Classroom use	Classification use
Administration procedures	Tester discretion allowed	Strict protocol followed
Tester qualifications	Minimal training needed	Extensive training needed
Comparisons	Skill growth in child	Normative comparisons among children or criterion-based decisions

tions. The term *reliability* refers to this desired consistency, or stability, of assessment results. Borrowing an analogy from McKenna and Stahl (2003), McDonald's is known for the reliability of their hamburgers—they are consistent whether you buy them in Alabama or Alaska! There are two types of reliability that are of particular concern to teachers. One type, *test–retest reliability*, relates to the consistency of performance over repeated administrations of the same test. Test–retest reliability tells us how confident we can be that our instrument will provide similar results if a child took the same test more than once. We would have less confidence in a test of fluency if it indicated that a child was a fluent reader one day and a disfluent one the next. A second type of reliability is *alternate-forms reliability*. Many tests have more than one form. Alternate form reliability compares two forms of the same test to ensure that they measure a skill in the same way. On oral reading fluency tests, this stipulation means that the passages should have approximately the same difficulty level from form to form. This type of reliability allows children to be retested after short periods of time without having to worry that their gains in performance are simply due to familiarity with the test. Obviously, if the child has read the passages on a test of oral reading fluency before, it is likely that he or she will do better on a second reading. As with test–retest reliability, you would have less confidence in the test if children who scored highly on one form of the test scored poorly on another form of the same test.

Reliability information is generally computed as a correlation and expressed as a number between 1 and 0. A reliability index of 1.0 indicates a "perfectly" reliable measurement, and a reliability index of 0 represents a completely unreliable instrument. You should expect a reliability figure of at least .80. You can usually find these numbers in the test manual, and you should use them to help you determine how consistent your learners' results will be.

Though a test may provide similar results each time it is administered, that reliability does not guarantee that it is measuring the kind of information that is useful for making important educational decisions. Thus, a second measure of good quality is a test's *validity*, which refers to the extent to which you can reasonably base decisions about a learner's abilities on the results of a particular test. In other words, it is actually measuring what it claims to measure. For example, if the results of a fluency test indicate that a child is ready to tackle more difficult material, you would have more confidence in the validity of the test if you found that the child actually could handle more difficult material. Unlike reliability data, test validation is never fully achieved. Instead it represents a process of acquiring evidence over different uses, along with research on the characteristics of the test to support its use.

We consider three types of validity evidence to be most important: *construct validity*, *content validity*, and *criterion* (predictive) *validity*. Whenever a test is administered, we want to be sure that it is actually measuring what it was designed to measure. This assurance, or *construct validity*, reflects the degree to which a test measures the skill or trait of interest. In many respects, construct validity is based upon a theoretical argument that clearly establishes what the skill is and is not, and to what other skills the skill being tested should be (theoretically) related. For oral reading fluency, construct validity would largely depend on our definition of fluency (as noted in Chapter 1). If our definition of fluency was "rate-limited comprehension," we would expect a measure of comprehension as well as measures of rate and accuracy. If our definition included "reading with expression," we would expect to find a measure of expression as well as rate and accuracy.

Just because a test publisher claims that a particular test measures reading fluency does not mean that it actually does so in a meaningful way. An example might help to clarify this point. The Woodcock–Johnson Tests of Achievement—Third Edition (Woodcock, McGrew, & Mather, 2001) has a Reading Fluency subtest that requires a student to read silently and verify the truth of as many single-sentence statements as possible within 3 minutes. An item found in this subtest might look something like the following: *The sky is blue* Y or N. Children are provided with a list of such items. Although this task does appear to measure speed of reading and processing of written text, you might reasonably question the test's relevance for evaluating reading fluency. It is entirely possible that a student could perform well on this test and still not be able to read more extensive connected text in a fluent way. You will simply have to use your best professional judgment, based on your knowledge of the topic, to decide whether the test is appropriately measuring fluency. Thus, it is important to become knowledgeable about both the skill and the specific test content when making decisions about your students' abilities on the basis of such test scores.

Content validity is concerned with the extent to which a test appropriately samples a given topic. Thus, it is important that a fluency test assess the skills that make up oral reading fluency (i.e., accurate, automatic, and expressive reading). In the above example, we do not know much about the child's reading accuracy or his or her ability to read with expression. In that sense, the test does not have content that adequately samples the topic of reading fluency.

Finally, *predictive validity* indicates the degree to which the score on a test predicts a child's score in some related area. With regard to fluency, we might want to consider how well our chosen test of fluency predicts how well the child does on local and state tests of reading achievement. This ability to predict may depend greatly on the characteristics of the local or state tests in addition to the characteristics of our test of fluency.

What Are the Main Types of Standardized Assessments?

There are different types of standardized tests, each with distinct purposes. Two possible purposes are common: (1) to distinguish among individuals on a given skill, and (2) to provide scores that describe levels of proficiency in a given skill. That is, some tests (norm-referenced tests) are created so that an individual's score on a given skill can be compared with the scores of others (e.g., the SATs); alternatively, other tests (criterion-referenced tests) are designed to measure whether an individual has "enough" skill or knowledge based on a set criteria (e.g., does a child know all the letters of the alphabet?). This is an important distinction because a test that is designed to qualify students for a gifted language arts class, say, would differ considerably from a test designed to assess minimum competency in reading fluency (i.e., does this child read fluently enough to do well in reading in the next grade?). Therefore, being clear about the purpose of the test is necessary to ensure that the standardized test is appropriate for your goals.

Norm-Referenced Assessment

Norm-referenced tests are those in which scores are used to compare children of the same age or grade with other children. *Norm-referenced assessment* allows you to determine the relative rank of a child in relation to his or her peers across the country. There are a dizzying array of scores that are produced by norm-referenced measures, including raw scores, *standard scores*, *scaled scores*, percentile ranks, age equivalents, and grade equivalents. To make this concept concrete, let's focus on an actual fluency measure, the Gray Oral Reading Test–4 (GORT-4; Wiederholt & Bryant, 2001), perhaps the most well-known and widely used norm-referenced standardized measure of oral reading ability.

The GORT-4 is designed for students ages 6 years, 0 months to 18 years, 11 months. The test consists of two parallel forms, each containing 14 developmentally sequenced reading passages with five comprehension questions following each passage. Reading ability is assessed for Rate, Accuracy, Fluency (i.e., the combination of Rate and Accuracy scores), and Comprehension. *Scaled scores* with a mean, or average, of 10 and a *standard deviation* of 3 are provided for each of these component areas. Further, the Fluency and Comprehension Scale scores can be combined to form an overall oral reading quotient (ORQ). The ORQ is represented by a standard score with a mean of 100 and a standard deviation of 15. But what exactly do these scores mean?

INTERPRETING NORM-REFERENCED MEASURES

We can begin to understand norm-referenced score interpretation with a discussion of the "normal," or bell-shaped, distribution. The *normal distri-*

bution conveys the idea that most children perform similarly on any given test but that there are fewer children who are exceptional. The normal distribution represents a theoretical frequency distribution wherein typical children's scores are concentrated near the center (or mean) and exceptional children's scores (either in a good way or a bad way) decrease in frequency as the distance from the mean increases. As you can see in Figure 8.2, there are a few people with very low scores, a few with very high scores, and many with scores that are about average.

The most common score reported for norm-referenced standardized measures is the standard score. Basically, a *standard score* is a *raw score* (defined as the total number of points earned) converted to a normal distribution with a set mean and standard deviation that has equal units along the scale. A standard deviation (*SD*) is a measure of the average distance of the test scores from the mean. Given a normal distribution, the standard deviation always divides up the same proportion of the distribution. As you can see in Figure 8.2, ± 1 *SD* always includes approximately 68% of children's scores, ± 2 *SD* always includes approximately 95% of children's scores, and so on. Let's use an example. The GORT-4 ORQ, for instance, has a mean of 100 and an *SD* of 15. Scores that are located within 1 *SD* from the mean in either direction are considered to be indicative of average performance. Thus, given a mean of 100, scores between 85 and 115 (which include roughly 68% of the population) are considered to be within the average range. Scores between 115 and 130, which are located between 1 and 2 *SD*s above the mean, are considered to be in the above-average range. Scores above 130 (more than 2 *SD*s above the mean) are considered to be in the superior range. The converse of this pattern is that scores between 70 and 85 are considered below average, and scores below 70 are indicative of significantly below-average achievement. Figure 8.3 shows this distribution using standard scores that correspond to the deviations explained above.

Scaled scores are another common type of standard score that have been popularized for use with specific subtests or domains (e.g., Rate, Accuracy, Fluency, and Comprehension). Scaled scores on the GORT-4

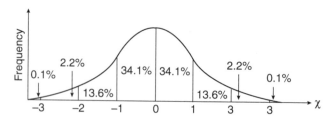

FIGURE 8.2. Depiction of the normal distribution using standard deviations.

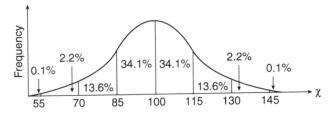

FIGURE 8.3. Depiction of the normal distribution using standard scores.

have a mean of 10 and an *SD* of 3. These scores are particularly useful because they facilitate interpretation of a child's actual skills. On these subtests, scores between 7 and 13 are considered to be within the average range. Scores between 13 and 16 are considered to be above average, with scores above 16 considered superior. Likewise, scores between 4 and 7 are considered below average, and scores below 4 are significantly below average.

A *percentile rank* gives the relative position of a particular child's score in reference to his or her peers. Percentile ranks are often useful for test interpretation because they facilitate communication about a child's performance with parents and other individuals who may not have extensive measurement backgrounds. For example, it is rather easy for a parent or educator to understand that a percentile rank of 50 indicates that the child's performance was better than roughly 50% of the other performances in the norm group and worse than roughly 50% of scores in the norm group. One major disadvantage of percentile ranks, however, is that they have unequal units along their scale (unlike standard scores). That is, because the greatest percentage of scores in the normal distribution is located in the center, percentile ranks overemphasize differences in scores that are located in the middle of the distribution and underemphasize score differences in the tails of the distribution. For instance, a standard score of 100 obtained on the GORT-ORQ corresponds to the 50th percentile, and a score of 105 corresponds to the 65th percentile. Thus, within the center of the distribution a relatively small standard score difference looks much larger if expressed in percentile ranks. However, because far fewer people score at the extreme ends of the distribution, the reverse is true. At the tails of the distribution, large score differences are not reflected when interpreted using percentile ranks. For example, the difference between the 1st and 5th percentiles looks quite small but is actually a difference of 10 standard score points (scores of 66 and 76, respectively). The reason we bring up this point is because this characteristic of percentile ranks can cause problems when interpreting tests under certain circumstances. A standard score of 90, for example, corresponds to the 25th percentile. Although we know from earlier discussion that such a score is well within the average range, it is often difficult to convince a parent that his or her child is functioning appropriately if you say that the child is performing at the 25th percentile. Therefore, we recommend that percentile ranks not be used to interpret performance when they have the potential to be misleading.

Tests makers often also produce developmental scores called *age* and *grade equivalents*. Although these scores, particularly grade equivalents, are often used by educators to describe the performance of their students, they are perhaps the most problematic of all scores reported and the most prone to misinterpretation. Suppose that one of your students obtained a fluency grade equivalent score of 6.0. It is common that this score be interpreted to mean that the student is performing at a sixth-grade level. However, a third-grade student who obtains a grade equivalent score of 6.0 has not necessarily mastered the skills that would be covered through the sixth grade. Instead, this score is an estimate of the score a typical sixth-grade student would achieve if he or she took the same test that the third grader was given. Of course, since sixth graders take only the sixth-grade test, this is only an estimate. Thus, grade equivalents are *not* an indicator of the level of curricular knowledge. Given these possible misconceptions, we find them to be of little value and recommend that they not be used.

Let's consider Tierra, a third grader who is experiencing difficulties with reading. She appears to have acquired adequate basic reading skills because she can read common sight words and seems to have acceptable decoding skills. However, Tierra's reading fell apart when reading connected text. After assessing her fluency informally, Tierra's teacher was concerned about more serious reading difficulties and referred her for additional standardized testing. Tierra was administered the GORT-4 to assess her oral reading ability, including oral reading rate, accuracy, fluency, and comprehension skills. Her scores are presented in Table 8.5.

Tierra's performance yielded an ORQ of 79 (8th percentile), which fell in the below-average range. Scores for Rate, Accuracy, Fluency, and Comprehension Scales were all significantly below average as well. Although reading rate may be affected by other factors (such as a general processing speed deficit), Tierra exhibited additional difficulties in the accuracy of reading connected text and poor comprehension skills. Taken together, these scores indicate that Tierra does, indeed, have very poor reading fluency that will need considerable remediation.

Criterion-Referenced Assessment

Criterion-referenced tests are most often used to determine competence or mastery over specific material. Thus, a child's score is based not on how he or she performs in comparison to others, but on how the individual does in relation to specific expectations about what he or she is supposed to know,

TABLE 8.5. Tierra's Scores on Standardized Assessments of Reading Fluency

	Gray Oral Reading Test-4	
	Scaled Scores	Percentile Rank
Rate	4	2
Accuracy	4	2
Fluency	3	1
Comprehension	5	5
	Standard Score	Percentile Rank
GORT-4 Oral Reading Quotient	79	8
	DIBELS	
	Instructional Category	Percentile Rank
Oral Reading Fluency	At-Risk	2
	(may need intensive instructional support)	

or, in the case of fluency, how quickly and accurately he or she is expected to read at that particular point in the school year. The Dynamic Indicators of Basic Early Literacy Skills–Sixth Edition (DIBELS; Good & Kaminski, 2002), for example, are a set of criterion-referenced, individually administered measures of early literacy development. The DIBELS Oral Reading Fluency (ORF) measure was designed to assess a child's accuracy and reading fluency with grade-level-connected text for grades 1–5 and above. The DIBELS passages are leveled according to grade. A different set of three passages exists for each benchmark assessment (fall, winter, and spring) in each grade. Performance is measured by having the students read each passage aloud for 1 minute and recording the total number of words read correctly. When administering all three passages, the median (or middle) score is used as an index of the child's oral reading rate. Students are then classified into one of three instructional categories (low risk, some risk, at risk) based on the benchmark goals for cwpm reported by the test authors.

As can be seen in Table 8.5, the reading specialist carried out a DIBELS assessment of Tierra's ORF skills and found that the results mirrored those of the GORT-4, indicating that Tierra may need considerable intensive instructional support for fluency. The DIBELS assessments and norm tables are free and available online (*www.dibels.uoregon.edu*).

CLOSING THOUGHTS

In this chapter we have presented what we believe are the most useful methods for assessing your students' reading fluency. Similarly, we feel comfortable recommending that you tailor your instructional goals based on the results of these assessments. We also provided a general discussion of key measurement concepts in education and introduced two specific standardized measurement tools that are likely to be used by your colleagues within the school setting. Whether the purpose is to inform instructional decisions in the classroom or to make special education placements, there are a number of options available for fluency assessment. Knowledge of the variety of assessments will not only help you become a more effective teacher but will also assist you in understanding how a particular student may be performing relative to other students. In short, understanding these assessments will help you be a better teacher.

REFERENCES

Burns, M. K., MacQuarrie, L. L., & Campbell, D. T. (1999). The difference between curriculum- based assessment and curriculum-based measurement: A focus on purpose and result. *ASP Communiqué, 27*, 6. Available at *nasponline.org/publications/cq276cba.html.*

Clay, M. M. (2002). *An observation survey of early literacy achievement* (2nd ed.). Portsmouth, NH: Heinemann.

Dowhower, S. L. (1989). Repeated reading: Research into practice. *The Reading Teacher, 42*, 502–507.

Fountas, I. C., & Pinnell, G. S. (1996). *Guided reading: Good first teaching for all children.* Portsmouth, NH: Heinemann.

Good, R. H., & Kaminski, R. A. (2002). *Dynamic indicators of basic early literacy skills* (6th ed.). Eugene: University of Oregon.

Gunning, T. G. (1998). *Best books for beginning readers.* Boston: Allyn & Bacon.

Hasbrouck, J. E., & Tindal, G. (2006). Oral reading fluency norms: A valuable assessment tool for reading teachers. *The Reading Teacher, 59*(7), 636–644.

Kuhn, M. R., & Stahl, S. (2003). Fluency: A review of developmental and remedial strategies. *Journal of Educational Psychology, 95*, 1–19.

McKenna, M. C., & Stahl, S. A. (2003). *Assessment for reading instruction.* New York: Guilford Press.

Rasinksi, T. V. (2003). *The fluent reader: Oral reading strategies for building word recognition, fluency, and comprehension.* New York: Scholastic Professional Books.

Rasinski, T. V. (2004). *Assessing reading fluency.* Honolulu: Pacific Resources for Education and Learning. Retrieved September 7, 2006, from *www.prel.org/products/re_/assessing-fluency.htm.*

Reutzel, D. R. (2003, May). *Fluency: What is it? how to assess it? how to develop it!* Paper presented at the annual meeting of the International Reading Association, Orlando, FL.

Schwanenflugel, P. J., Meisinger, E., Wisenbaker, J. M., Kuhn, M. R., Strauss, G. P., & Morris, R. D. (2006). Becoming a fluent and automatic reader in the early elementary school years. *Reading Research Quarterly, 41*(4), 496–522.

White, S. (1995). *Listening to children read aloud*. Washington, DC: National Center for Education Statistics.

Wiederholt, J. L., & Bryant, B. R. (2001). *Gray Oral Reading Tests—Fourth Edition*. Austin, TX: PRO-ED.

Woodcock, R. W., McGrew, K. S., & Mather, N. (2001). *Woodcock–Johnson III Tests of Achievement*. Itasca, IL: Riverside.

Zutell, J., & Rasinski, T. V. (1991). Training teachers to attend to their students' oral reading fluency. *Theory into Practice, 30,* 211–217.

CHAPTER 9

The Word Zone Fluency Curriculum
An Alternative Approach

ELFRIEDA H. HIEBERT

THIS CHAPTER DESCRIBES:

- The importance of attending to the words in texts that students read as part of repeated and guided reading fluency instruction.
- A fluency curriculum that consists of high-frequency words and words with consistent rimes (i.e., vowel and consonant patterns) that appear frequently in texts for young children.
- Evidence that the fluency levels of beginning and struggling readers are supported when repeated and guided reading occurs with texts that follow the fluency curriculum.
- Sources for texts that give students experiences with the fluency curriculum.

Young children participate in reading long before they are said to be reading. They listen and follow along as adults read to them. Often, they pick out words that they know in a book. For children to be described as reading, however, they need to be able to decipher the words in written texts and understand the ideas represented by the words. Children differ enormously, both at particular points in their development and within an age group, in their ability to read the same text. Consider, for example, how two second graders read a text that is a benchmark of mid-second-grade reading on a widely used oral reading assessment (Dynamic Indicators of Basic Early Literacy Skills [DIBELS]; Good & Kaminski, 1996):

> My parents decided we were just too crowded in our apartment and we needed more room. At our new house my brother and I won't have to share a room anymore. The house has two bathrooms so we won't have to stand in line to use the bathroom anymore. (Good & Kaminski, 1996, p. 11)

The first child, Jasmine, reads this excerpt at the rate of approximately 80 correct words per minute (cwpm), meaning that she is at the 50th percentile in oral reading fluency (Hasbrouck & Tindal, 2006). There are only a handful of words on which Jasmine hesitates, words such as *anymore, apartment,* and *bathroom.* Jasmine's reading shows that a fluent reader in an age cohort does not read every word in the text automatically. However, because she recognizes a sufficient number of the words in the text automatically, she can sustain her understanding of the text when attending to new, unknown words.

Marc, a student at the 15th percentile of a mid-second-grade age cohort, reads the same passage at 33 cwpm. After he pauses for 5 seconds on the words *parents, decided, crowded,* and *apartment,* Marc's teacher steps in and pronounces these words for him. Marc recognizes the words *share* and *brother* only after pausing and studying the words. He makes several attempts at *bathrooms* and *anymore,* finally coming up with the correct words. The number of words that Marc does not recognize automatically means that his rate of reading is sufficiently slow to impede comprehension. Marc is an example of a disfluent reader and is likely to be labeled a struggling reader in subsequent grades.

By the middle of second grade, Jasmine has developed automatic recognition of words that occur frequently in written language—a proficiency that is part of fluency. By contrast, Marc has trouble with words that appear frequently in written English, such as *share, brother, decided, parents,* and *crowded.* To use context and phonics effectively to recognize rarer words in the texts he has to read, Marc needs to automatically recognize the words that comprise the bulk of texts. In my thinking about fluency, these highly and moderately frequent words are what make up the word zone "fluency curriculum."

This chapter addresses three questions:

1. What is the word zone fluency curriculum?
2. How do texts affect students' fluency?
3. Where can teachers find texts that support students' fluency?

WHAT IS THE WORD ZONE FLUENCY CURRICULUM?

In the state standards of the two largest U.S. states, California and Texas, which are the home to approximately one-fifth of the nation's students, the terms *grade-appropriate* and *grade-level text* are used but never defined, leaving their meanings unclear. This lack of clarity becomes apparent when the grade levels assigned to the same texts are compared. For example, *Officer Buckle and Gloria* (Rathman, 1995) is considered a middle-of-the-second-grade text of the most widely used program in California (Cooper et al., 2003). By contrast, this very same text also appears in the middle of the third-grade textbook of the most widely used program in Texas (Farr et al., 2001). What accounts for this discrepancy? It is unclear. Neither the California nor Texas state standards provide any information that would lead to an understanding of this full year difference in grade-appropriate texts.

Insight into the words that make up the bulk of texts comes from analyses of textbooks. The most recent of these, conducted by Zeno, Ivens, Millard, and Duvvuri (1995), sampled 17.25 million words that came from schoolbooks of different content areas from kindergarten through college. Zeno et al. were able to estimate the number of times unique or different words can be expected to appear in a sample of 1 million words. From this database, I identified seven *word zones* (Hiebert, 2005a), which appear in Table 9.1. The word zones differ in size and also in the number of times the words in them can be expected to appear in a million-word sample of words. The number of words in the highly frequent zones is relatively small (930) compared to the number of words in the least frequent zone (135,000).

I use this concept of word zones to think about the texts in popular standardized tests of reading fluency, such as the Gray Oral Reading Test discussed earlier (GORT, see Chapter 8; Wiederholt & Bryant, 2001).

TABLE 9.1. Word Zones for 160,000 Unique Words

Word zone	Label for zone or group of zones	Number of unique words	Percentage of total words (cumulative)	Examples of words
0	}Highly frequent	107	48	*the, of*
1		203	57	*away, between*
2		610	67	*day, different*
3	}Moderately frequent	1,676	74	*tree, travel*
4		2,980	79	*invited, blanket*
5	}Rare	13,882	87	*butterfly, frosting*
6		135,473	100	*jeered, parasol*

Note. Based on Zeno et al. (1995).

Through grade 2, 97% or more of the words on the GORT come from zones 0–2. By the end of grade 4, highly frequent words still account for a high percentage (86%), with moderately frequent words accounting for 11% and rare words for only 2%. Rare words do not account for an appreciable percentage of words (31–38%) until grades 9 and 10. At least in measuring oral reading fluency on a widely used measure such as the GORT, automatic recognition of highly frequent words figures heavily.

This is no accident. William S. Gray, the conceptual source of the GORT and also of the *Dick and Jane* readers (Gray, Monroe, Artley, Arbuthnot, & Gray, 1956), believed that proficient reading depended on learning high-frequency words. Gray was right in that the frequency rating of a word influences readers' recognition of words (Rayner, 1977). In his exclusive focus on highly frequent words, Gray failed to recognize the importance of phonetically regular words. Numerous rimes (i.e., vowels and subsequent consonants) appear consistently in a large number of words that occur commonly in texts for young children (Wylie & Durrell, 1970). An example of a consistent, common rime is *-at*, which appears in five words among the 1,000 most-frequent words—*at, that, cat, hat,* and *sat*— as well as an additional four words among the 5,000 most-frequent words—*bat, fat, flat, rat.* Beginning readers recognize words with consistent, common rimes more readily than words that have inconsistent or infrequent rimes (Thompson, Cottrell, & Fletcher-Flinn, 1996). Fluent reading depends on automatic recognition of common, consistent letter–sound patterns *and* of high-frequency words.

In this chapter, I describe a model of fluency development that addresses the features of text that students read as part of fluency instruction as well as instructional activities such as guided and repeated reading. Similar to Fluency-Oriented Reading Instruction (FORI; Stahl & Heubach, 2005) and Wide Reading instruction that underlie most of the chapters in this volume, the model discussed in this chapter emphasizes guided and repeated reading as important mechanisms in the development of fluency. Unlike the FORI and Wide Reading perspective, which emphasize that only grade-level texts should be used for fluency, this model contends that the specific characteristics of the words in the texts used for guided and repeated practice matter. It is my position that *texts*, not just instructional activities, are important factors in the instruction of fluency.

In the TExT (text elements by task) model (Hiebert, 2002), the percentage of words within a text that comes from different word zones and that have particular vowel patterns is used to establish how easy or difficult that text is for beginning and struggling readers. The curriculum moves from texts with high percentages of words with simple vowel patterns and highly frequent words to texts with progressively more complex vowel patterns and less frequent words. For simplicity, to distinguish it from the other fluency curriculums presented in this book, I refer to this curriculum as the "word zone" curriculum. The curriculum is presented in Table 9.2.

The word zone fluency curriculum in Table 9.2 is proposed as a source for selecting texts for fluency practice for beginning and struggling readers. According to the TExT model, beginning and struggling readers need a substantial amount of practice with carefully chosen texts that have a large percentage of words from particular zones and with particular vowel and syllabic patterns. Texts that have a high proportion of high-frequency words and simple vowels in one-syllable words also are likely to have few words that are rare and multisyllabic (i.e., difficult to recognize for beginning and struggling readers).

The curriculum based on the TExT model is not intended as a guide in the selection of texts for all students, such as those who are proficient readers even as first or second graders. Instead, it is intended as a guide for choosing texts for children who are not proficient grade-level readers. Further, although beginning and struggling readers may benefit from receiving a number of texts at these levels, they should not be limited to reading only texts that fall within this range. However, without automatic recognition of the words that account for large percentages of texts (i.e., the word zones that are lower in the curriculum and have simple, rather than complex or variant, vowel patterns), children's ability to glean meaning from the reading of text will be jeopardized. Students who aren't proficient grade-level readers will need many experiences with texts in which these two types of words (i.e., high-frequency and one-syllable words) account for the majority of the words in the texts.

TABLE 9.2. Word Zone Fluency Curriculum

	High-frequency content	Phonics and syllabic content	Morphological content
A	300 most frequent words	Short and long vowels	Simple inflected endings (*ed, ing, s, es, 's*)
B	500 most frequent words	Short, long and *r*-controlled vowels	
C	1,000 most frequent words	All monosyllabic words	
D	1,000 most frequent words	Two-syllable compound words with at least one root from 1,000 most frequent words	Prefixes: *un, a* Suffixes: *er, est, ly, y* (with doubling of final consonant)
E	2,500 most frequent words		
F	5,000 most frequent words		

HOW DO TEXTS AFFECT STUDENTS' FLUENCY?

In this section, I first describe the features of texts that children read in current curricula. Second, I summarize research on which texts have been used in successful fluency interventions. Finally, I present a project I have carried out in which texts that emphasize the fluency curriculum have been developed and tested.

Features of Current Texts and the Fluency Curriculum

The distributions of the words in texts that students commonly encounter in school reading instruction are given in Table 9.3, and excerpts from these texts appear in Table 9.4. The texts include (1) those in a widely used basal reading program (Cooper et al., 2003), such as the FORI intervention (Kuhn et al., 2006); (2) texts used in the Wide Reading intervention, described in chapters throughout this volume and in Kuhn et al. (2006); (3) decodable texts; (4) high-interest/low-vocabulary (HI/LV) texts; (5) texts created from the fluency curriculum in Table 9.2 ("scaffolded" texts); and (6) science textbooks. In addition, the features of texts from the widely used assessment that introduced the chapter and those from a historical basal reading program (McKee, Harrison, McCowen, Lehr, & Durr, 1966)

TABLE 9.3. Number of New, Unique Words of Particular Types per 100 Words of Text

Text type	New, unique words per 100 words	Highly frequent words	Monosyllabic words (moderately frequent and rare)	Multisyllabic words (Multisyllabic moderately frequent and rare)	Multisyllabic words (moderately frequent and rare): Single appearing
Assessment (DIBELS)	27	20	3	4	2
Literature anthology	27	18	3	6	4
Wide Reading	27	19	5	3	2
Decodable text	26	18	6	2	0
High-interest/ low-vocabulary	17	12	3	2	1
Science textbook	17	12	2	3	1
Scaffolded text	17	14	2	1	0
Historical basal	26	20	3	3	2

TABLE 9.4. Excerpts from Texts Used for Reading Instruction

Excerpt No.	Source of text	Text excerpt
1a	Literature anthology (passage 1)	"Officer Buckle knew more safety tips than anyone else in Napville. Every time he thought of a new one, he thumbtacked it to his bulletin board. Safety Tip #77 NEVER stand on a SWIVEL CHAIR. Officer Buckle shared his safety tips with the students at Napville School. Nobody ever listened. Sometimes there was snoring" (Rathman, 1995).
1b	Literature anthology (passage 2)	"Ants do all kinds of things together. They pass pieces of food to one another. Sometimes they even carry each other around. Some jobs are too big for one ant. That's when ants team up. A bunch of little ants working together can carry a big dead bug" (Stefoff, 1998).
2	Wide Reading intervention	" 'Seth!' said Al. 'That does it! You sit in the stands! Do not bother me!' Seth went to sit in the stands. But it was no fun just sitting still. It was dull. He began to jump on the steps. Then he spotted the hot drink stand. Seth ran to the stand" (Rowland, 1982).
3	Decodable text	"At the town meeting, Bart Horn stood up. 'I have something important to say this morning,' he told the town board. 'We feel that a town named Parkdale needs a park.' Doctor Short nodded. So did Miss Martin. 'Pardon me,' said Cora Barkway, 'but how will we pay for this park?' " (Cooper et al., 2003).
4	High-interest/ low-vocabulary	" 'I can play by myself, Stanley. I don't need you, Stanley. And I mean it, Stanley. I am having a lot of fun. A lot of fun. I am making a great thing, Stanley. A really, truly great thing. And when it is done, you will want to see it, Stanley' " (Bonsall, 1984).
5	Science textbook	"All these objects are solids. They are different in color, size, and shape. They have different textures. A texture is the way something feels. Solids are alike in some important ways. Each one has its own size and shape. A solid will not change in size or shape unless you do something such as cut, bend, or break it" (Badders et al., 2000).
6	Scaffolded text	"George Washington Carver was a scientist who knew about plants. He learned that soil wears out when farmers grow the same crop every year. When soil wears out, crops are poor. George Washington Carver showed farmers how to grow one crop in one year. Then they would grow a different crop in the next year" (Hiebert, 2003).
7	Historical basal	"It had snowed in the night. Tim Baker could tell that it had without looking out of his bedroom window. There was always a bright whiteness about the daylight when the world was deep in snow. Tim lay in bed and thought about what he would do" (McKee et al., 1966).

are included. All of the texts are at a second-grade level because weekly fluency development is especially rapid at this level relative to other grades—approximately 1.5 words per week (Fuchs, Fuchs, Hamlett, Walz, & Germann, 1993). Each program was represented by a similar-size sample of 200 words from 10 different texts, for a total of 2,000 words per program.

A feature that influences text difficulty for developing and struggling readers is represented in the second column of Table 9.3: the number of *new, unique* words per 100 words. This figure indicates the rate of appearance of new, unique words for each new set of 100 words that have not appeared previously in the *second-grade* portion of the program. It is likely that some of these unique words—at least those that are among the first 100–300 most-frequent words in written English, appeared in the first-grade texts of this program. However, because many of the words that appear in the first-grade core reading programs, beyond the 100–300 most-frequent words, appear a single time (Foorman, Francis, Davidson, Harm, & Griffin, 2004), many of the new, unique words in the second-grade program will be new to developing and struggling readers. For developing and struggling readers, the appearance of each unfamiliar word requires attention.

As shown in Table 9.3, the texts are of two types. Assessment, literature anthology, Wide Reading, and decodable texts have around 26–27 new, unique words per 100. By contrast, HI/LV, science textbooks, and scaffolded texts have 17. Moreover, each word is repeated an average of 3.7 times in the first group of tests and 5.9 times in the other texts.

For beginning and struggling readers, the rate of introduction and repetition of words is especially challenging when percentages of new, unique words are moderately frequent or even rare. In all of the texts, except for the anthology, new words that are less frequent *and* multisyllabic range from 1 to 3 words per 100 words of text. If students can recognize highly frequent and single-syllable words, these texts will be at the independent level (98–100%) or high end of instructional level (95–97%) (Betts, 1946). After several rereadings of such texts, students should be reading the texts smoothly and facilely.

For those students who are not automatic with highly frequent words, texts such as those in the anthology with six infrequent, multisyllabic words will fall within their frustration level. Even after guidance and several readings, many second-grade students will be unable to recognize six new, infrequent, multisyllabic words. This challenge is exacerbated by single appearances of many of these words (see Table 9.3). The lack of repetition and the density of the rare multisyllabic words make it unlikely that struggling and beginning readers will learn even a small percentage of them.

Some have suggested that texts that are difficult for students—even ones at their frustration levels—should be used for fluency practice (Snow,

Griffin, & Burns, 2005). However, the majority of U.S. students, such as Marc, for whom the typical grade-level texts are at frustration level, do not display fluency even on the texts of tests that are easier than their instructional texts. As can be seen in Table 9.3, the mid-second-grade texts of the DIBELS (Good & Kaminski, 1996) benchmark assessments resemble the decodable, HI/LV, science, and scaffolded texts, not the anthology texts, in their percentage of highly and moderately frequent words and of rare single-appearing words. Even though the DIBELS texts are easier than the anthology texts that most U.S. second graders read for instruction, students such as Marc read neither the highly frequent nor moderately frequent-to-rare words automatically on the assessment. Even for students who are at the 50th percentile in oral reading fluency, such as Jasmine, a text with six new, multisyllabic words in every 100 words may place them at frustration level. In contrast, texts with one or two new words allow attention to smooth, automatic reading of the words that make up the majority of texts. This automaticity with core words supports students' capacity to attend to less frequent, multisyllabic words in future texts.

Research on Texts in Fluency Interventions

I believe that the fluency of primary-level readers is supported when their repeated and guided reading occurs with texts that have a high percentage of highly frequent or phonetically regular, monosyllabic words and low percentages of new, multisyllabic words. The first piece of evidence comes from an analysis that Charles Fisher and I conducted of the texts in the fluency studies reviewed by the National Reading Panel (NRP; National Institute of Child Health and Human Development, 2000). Our analysis of the original reports of the 16 studies in the NRP meta-analysis on fluency showed that three-quarters of the studies used texts with a high percentage of highly frequent words and a low percentage of rare multisyllabic words (Hiebert & Fisher, 2005). Of the handful of studies using texts with a relatively high percentage of rare multisyllabic words and a relatively lower percentage of highly frequent words, only one reported a fluency outcome—and it was not significant. Thus, the effect size for fluency reported by the NRP came from the studies using text types with some level of controlled vocabulary.

The studies in the NRP (National Institute of Child Health and Human Development, 2000) meta-analysis of fluency compared different instructional techniques with the same kinds of texts, so the effects on fluency of different kinds of texts were not examined. Among the few studies where texts have been varied, Rashotte and Torgesen (1985) found that repeated reading resulted in improved reading rate only when students read stories with high percentages of shared words (most of which were highly frequent words). Similarly, Faulkner and Levy (1994) found that improvements in disfluent readers' reading rate and accuracy were linked to texts where words overlapped.

Identifying and Designing Texts That Support the Fluency Curriculum

Many of the texts in the NRP (National Institute of Child Health and Human Development, 2000) studies that supported fluency came from old basal reading programs (Hiebert & Fisher, 2005). An example of such a text is summarized in Table 9.3—*Tim's Woods*. This text, although containing a high number of new, unique words per 100, has a low percentage of single-appearing multisyllabic words. However, whereas a text such as this may be accessible, its style and content does not engage students (Bruce, 1984). Some interventions—including some of the Wide Reading interventions described in other chapters in this volume—have used these texts to increase fluency levels. However, giving such texts to struggling readers in the 21st century is unlikely to generate the engagement that invites repeated and extended reading (Guthrie, Anderson, Alao, & Rinehart, 1999). Nor are these texts likely to support the development of background knowledge needed to be a proficient reader (Anderson & Pearson, 1984).

There are numerous sources, other than historical basal readers, that will support students in becoming automatic with highly frequent words and words with common, consistent vowel patterns, while at the same time providing content that engages students and extends their background knowledge. One source for fluency practice that may seem an unlikely one for teachers consists of the texts of science programs at least in the primary grades. As can be seen in Table 9.3, rare or moderately frequent words are often repeated in science texts. This repetition reflects the purpose of science texts. Authors of science texts are intent on communicating particular concepts related to topics such as *habitats of organisms* or the *nature of energy*. Because the aim is to communicate information about particular concepts, key concepts are repeated. In higher grades, science texts become substantially more difficult (building on the assumption that students have developed the facility with the science concepts and vocabulary of previous levels; Armstrong & Collier, 1990). However, in the primary grades, the hard words for basic concepts are repeated, as is evident in the summary of the text features in Table 9.3. This repetition of core words makes science texts ideal for fluency practice in the primary grades. At the same time, these experiences with science texts give students the opportunities they need to build background knowledge of nature and the world around them.

These characteristics of informational texts at the primary level, especially in science, were the basis for the creation of a set of informational texts (Hiebert, 2003) that were aimed at facilitating the automatic reading of highly and moderately frequent words. Because of the scaffolding of the fluency curriculum provided by these texts, they are referred to as "scaffolded texts." These scaffolded texts were written to give struggling readers systematic experiences with the fluency curriculum in Table 9.2. Approximately 98% of the words in the first level are among the 300 most frequent words or have the most common, consistent vowel patterns (i.e., short, long vowels) in monosyllabic words. By the third level of texts, approximately 98% of the words are either among the 1,000 most-frequent words or monosyllabic. By the final level, 98% of the words are among the 5,000 most-frequent words or are monosyllabic.

These texts were tested in several studies (Hiebert, 2005b, 2006), in which one group was involved in the FORI intervention (Stahl & Heubach, 2005) of using repeated and guided reading with texts from the basal reading anthology (see Tables 9.3 and 9.4), and the other group experienced repeated and guided reading with scaffolded texts. In both studies, the students whose repeated reading occurred with the scaffolded texts showed higher performances than students in the FORI intervention. Although differences between the two groups were not statistically different, the scaffolded texts group performed significantly better than a control group that read the literature in the basal reading program but without repeated reading (Hiebert, 2005b). The FORI group did not perform better than the control group.

In addition, classroom observations in the first study (Hiebert, 2005b) revealed that classes in the FORI intervention spent more than twice the time in repeated and guided reading as classes who received the scaffolded text intervention. In contrast, the scaffolded text intervention consumed approximately 15 minutes of language arts/reading blocks, leaving time for teachers to conduct guided reading lessons with the literature selections of the basal readers. Even with less time spent on repeated reading, students who did that reading with scaffolded texts had higher fluency gains than students who spent considerably longer periods of time in repeated and guided reading of less accessible text.

WHERE CAN TEACHERS FIND TEXTS THAT SUPPORT STUDENTS' FLUENCY?

Given that current anthologies of basal reading programs contain many rare multisyllabic words even in the first grade (Foorman et al., 2004), where can you, as teachers, find texts to support students' experiences with the fluency curriculum? It is to be hoped that writers and publishers would have recognized this need and provided appropriate texts for fluency practice. Recognition of the low fluency levels of many U.S. students is a recent phenomenon (e.g., Pinnell et al., 1995), however, and programs aimed at fluency are only beginning to appear on the market. What information should you use to evaluate new programs and, in the face of declining funds, choose the best texts from those already available in your class-rooms? Choices of texts for fluency instruction are informed by two sets of principles about texts: (a) guidelines on the features of accessible texts and (b) guidelines for reasons to read repeatedly.

Guidelines for Features of Accessible Texts

First, I believe that texts for fluency practice should be short. In the studies that were reviewed by the NRP (National Institute of Child Health and Human Development, 2000) subgroup on fluency, the typical text for a flu-ency session was between 50 and 150 words in length. There is a general perception, as fluency mandates have become more widespread, that entire texts of considerable length should be read repeatedly. In only one of the studies reviewed by the NRP were entire texts of approximately 500 or more words used for fluency practice—and in that study, students' fluency did not improve. This does not mean that an entire text of 500–600 words cannot be used for fluency practice over time. For example, a HI/LV text such as *And I Mean It, Stanley* (Bonsall, 1984) could be used for fluency activities over several sessions, with each 100-word segment providing the focus for another session.

From where in the word zone fluency curriculum should you choose books? In the intervention with scaffolded texts using the word zone metric (Hiebert, 2005b, 2006), I chose texts that were at the top end of students' instructional level and the low end of their independent level. Two unique words that fell outside the curriculum appeared within every 100 words. Students were given an assessment to determine the level of text on the flu-ency curriculum in Table 9.2 for which they could recognize the words at 97–98% levels of accuracy but lower than the 50th percentile for fluency.

General Guidelines for Reasons to Read Repeatedly

Just as young children who are acquiring a new skill can repeat a task over and over, young children who are learning to read can reread the same texts as they gain in competence. Whereas beginning readers may respond favorably to the task of reading a text repeatedly, the response of struggling readers to the repeated reading of difficult texts may not be as favorable. Struggling readers may need legitimate reasons to read texts repeatedly.

The goal of becoming a smoother, faster, and more knowledgeable reader is the underlying raison d'etre for repeated oral reading of texts. Guiding students to an awareness of their pace of reading provides a strong incentive for oral reading. Students can track their progress and set goals for reading (see Chapter 6 for a similar recommendation). However, too strong an emphasis on data gathering of reading rate can create pitfalls, as students focus on reading rapidly to the detriment of expression and meaning. Consequently, students benefit from tasks that require them to comprehend and learn from the texts that are used for fluency development. For example, in the scaffolded text intervention (Hiebert, 2005b, 2006), students kept a record of new vocabulary and information they intended to remember.

Reading with teachers or tutors who model fluent reading or monitor students' reading has been part of the repeated reading activity since Samuels's (1979) study. Teachers, tutors, or partners support students' attention to the text and ensure that repeated readings are productive. Repeated reading with technology, including voice-recognition on computers (Adams, 2006), is proving successful with students from the primary through high school grades. As voice-recognition on computers becomes more sophisticated, disfluent readers have increased opportunities for repeated reading that is monitored, provides models of proficient reading, and presents information on pronunciation and meaning.

Although the NRP (National Institute of Child Health and Human Development, 2000) identified repeated and guided oral reading as most effective in improving fluency, the long-term goal is for students to be fluent in silent reading. Considerable debate has centered around the failure of the NRP to locate empirical evidence validating the benefits of sustained silent reading on reading proficiencies, including fluency. Part of the explanation may lie with the typical implementation of silent reading in which students select their own texts and are not held accountable for what happens during the event. By contrast, Reutzel (2005) included a "scaffolded silent reading" treatment in a study of fluency. Students in this treatment read specified texts silently with particular tasks in mind. Reutzel reported that students in the scaffolded silent reading treatment had the same fluency gains as students in the repeated oral treatment.

In the scaffolded text intervention described earlier (Hiebert, 2005b, 2006), the repeated reading portion moves between silent and oral reading. Whether students are in an oral or silent phase of the repeated reading cycle, the teacher specifies the portion of text to be read, the amount of time to be spent reading, and the task to be accomplished with the text. The instructional cycle is oriented toward what students are learning and remembering from reading, not on simply reading faster or sounding better. Huxley (2006) found that although third graders gained in fluency over a 10-week intervention with the scaffolded texts, their most significant gains occurred in the retention of information about the content of the texts.

Places to Find Texts

Current anthologies of basal reading programs consist primarily of selections from children's literature that, as has been described, often contain relatively high percentages of rare multisyllabic words. But even among selections of children's literature, percentages of rare multisyllabic words vary. Informational texts within the basal anthology are especially good candidates for fluency practice, as is evident in the excerpt from *Ants* (Stefoff, 1998) in Table 9.4, which is part of the same basal reading unit as *Office Buckle and Gloria*. In this excerpt of *Ants*, there are no rare multisyllabic words. Further, once a selection in the basal anthology has been studied, a portion might be used for fluency practice.

At least at the second-grade level, there is likely another excellent source of fluency development in most basal reading anthologies: one or two selections from HI/LV texts such as the *Frog and Toad* or *Henry and Mudge* series. These texts have high percentages of highly frequent words and relatively low percentages of rare multisyllabic words (see Table 9.3). Within the teachers' manuals of basal programs, guidelines for instruction are the same for HI/LV texts as for any other text. However, with the knowledge that these texts were designed to emphasize highly frequent words, you might choose to reserve the HI/LV texts in your basal reading programs for fluency development. When a 500- to 600-word HI/LV text is segmented into chunks of about 100 words, you will have sufficient texts for five or more fluency sessions.

Another source of accessible texts for fluency practice is the decodables that are part of primary-level basal reading programs. The decodables that are part of the same unit as *Officer Buckle and Gloria* have the same percentage of rare words as the anthology. Unlike the rare words in the anthology, which tend to be multisyllabic, the rare words in the decodables are mostly monosyllabic. Some rare monosyllabic words, such as *tam* or *vat*, may not be in the known speaking or even listening vocabularies of second and third graders who are struggling readers. However, these words will be easier for many students to decode than most rare multisyllabic words, such as *penalty* and *auditorium* (words in the basal unit summarized in Table 9.3). When rare words can be pronounced and context can be used to make meaning of them (as is the case with some rare monosyllabic words), students may have the experiences they need to become more fluent.

The excerpt from *Ants* confirms another source of accessible texts for fluency development that has already been described: the textbooks of science programs. At least in the primary grades, science textbooks have features that make them less difficult than the texts of basal reading programs. Whereas rare words in literature are typically used a single time to capture a trait of a character or the circumstances of an event, rare words in science texts represent the concepts that are the focus of the text. As excerpts 1b and 5 in Table 9.4 illustrate, writers of science texts typically repeat rare words as they describe and elaborate upon the central concepts of the texts.

Finally, educators will find an increasing number of texts offered specifically for fluency development. Excerpt 6 in Table 9.4 indicates that texts can emphasize the fluency curriculum while conveying information in an engaging manner. As programs aimed at fluency come into the marketplace, be assured that the same principles should be applied to these texts as to any other set of texts. That is, texts should be evaluated from the vantage point of the opportunities provided with the fluency curriculum and the challenges inherent in significant numbers of rare multisyllabic words.

The ideas about fluency are not new (see, e.g., Huey, 1908), but the wide-scale recognition of the importance of fluency is new. The NRP (National Institute of Child Health and Human Development, 2000) based its conclusions on classroom *practices* for encouraging the development of fluency, not the *texts* that are most useful in implementing these practices. It is my view that, for disfluent readers, the texts that are read and reread for fluency practice need to have sufficiently high percentages of words within what I have called the "word zone fluency curriculum" and low percentages of rare words, especially multisyllabic ones. By using texts that emphasize the word zone fluency curriculum, educators can be assured that they are supporting their beginning and struggling readers on the road to fluent and meaningful reading.

REFERENCES

Adams, M. J. (2006). The promise of automatic speech recognition for fostering literacy growth in children and adults. In M. McKenna, L. Labbo, R. Kieffer, & D. Reinking (Eds.), *Handbook of literacy and technology* (Vol. 2, pp. 109–128). Hillsdale, NJ: Erlbaum.

Anderson, R. C., & Pearson, P. D. (1984). A schema-theoretic view of basic processes in reading comprehension. In P. D. Pearson, R. Barr, M. L. Kamil, & P. Mosenthal (Eds.), *Handbook of reading research* (Vol. 1, pp. 255–292). New York: Longman.

Armstrong, J. E., & Collier, G. E. (1990). *Science in biology: An introduction.* Prospect Heights, IL: Waveland Press.

Badders, W., Bethel, L. J., Fu, V., Peck, D., Sumners, C., & Valentino, C. (2000). *Houghton Mifflin science discoveryworks: California edition.* Boston: Houghton Mifflin.

Betts, E. (1946). *Foundations of reading instruction.* New York: American Book.

Bonsall, C. (1984). *And I mean it, Stanley.* New York: HarperTrophy.

Bruce, B. C. (1984). A new point of view on children's stories. In R. C. Anderson, J.

Osborn, & R. J. Tierney (Eds.), *Learning to read in American schools: Basal readers and content texts* (pp. 153–174). Hillsdale, NJ: Erlbaum.

Cooper, J. D., Pikulski, J. J., Ackerman, P. A., Au, K. H., Chard, D. J., Garcia, G. G., et al. (2003). *Houghton Mifflin reading: The nation's choice.* Boston: Houghton Mifflin.

Farr, R. C., Strickland, D. S., Beck, I. L., Abrahamson, R. F., Ada, A. F., Cullinan, B. E., et al. (2001). *Collections: Harcourt reading/language arts program.* Orlando, FL: Harcourt.

Faulkner, H. J., & Levy, B. A. (1994). How text difficulty and reader skill interact to produce differential reliance on word and content overlap in reading transfer. *Journal of Experimental Child Psychology, 58,* 1–24.

Foorman, B. R., Francis, D. J., Davidson, K. C., Harm, M. W., & Griffin, J. (2004). Variability in text features in six grade 1 basal reading programs. *Scientific Studies of Reading, 8,* 167–197.

Fuchs, L. S., Fuchs, D., Hamlett, C. L., Walz, L., & Germann, G. (1993). Formative evaluation of academic progress: How much growth can we expect? *School Psychology Review, 22*(1), 27–48.

Good, R. H., & Kaminski, R. A. (1996). *Dynamic Indicators of Basic Literacy Skills.* Eugene: University of Oregon.

Gray, W. S., Monroe, M., Artley, A. S., Arbuthnot, A. H., & Gray, L. (1956). *The new basic readers: Curriculum foundation series.* Chicago: Scott, Foresman.

Guthrie, J. T., Anderson, E., Alao, S., & Rinehart, J. (1999). Influences of concept-oriented reading instruction on strategy use and conceptual learning from text. *Elementary School Journal, 99*(4), 343–366.

Hasbrouck, J. E., & Tindal, G. (2006). Oral reading fluency norms: A valuable tool for reading teachers. *The Reading Teacher, 59,* 636–644.

Hiebert, E. H. (2002). Standards, assessment, and text difficulty. In A. E. Farstrup & S. J. Samuels (Eds.). *What research has to say about reading instruction* (3rd ed., pp. 337–369) Newark, DE: International Reading Association.

Hiebert, E. H. (2003). *QuickReads.* Parsippany, NJ: Pearson Learning Group.

Hiebert, E. H. (2005a). In pursuit of an effective, efficient vocabulary curriculum for the elementary grades. In E. H. Hiebert & M. Kamil (Eds.), *The teaching and learning of vocabulary: Bringing scientific research to practice* (pp. 243–263). Mahwah, NJ: Erlbaum.

Hiebert, E. H. (2005b). The effects of text difficulty on second graders' fluency development. *Reading Psychology, 26,* 1–27.

Hiebert, E. H. (2006). Becoming fluent: What difference do texts make? In S. J. Samuels & A. E. Farstrup (Eds.), *What research has to say about reading fluency* (pp. 204–226). Newark, DE: International Reading Association.

Hiebert, E. H., & Fisher, C. W. (2005). A review of the National Reading Panel's studies on fluency: On the role of text. *Elementary School Journal, 105,* 443–460.

Huey, E. B. (1968). *The psychology and pedagogy of reading.* Cambridge, MA: MIT Press. (Original work published 1908)

Huxley, A. (2006). *A text-based intervention of reading fluency, comprehension, and content knowledge.* Unpublished doctoral dissertation, University of Michigan, Ann Arbor, MI.

Kuhn, M., Schwanenflugel, P. J., Morris, R. D., Morrow, L. M., Woo, D., Messinger, E. B., et al. (2006). Teaching children to become fluent and automatic readers. *Journal of Library Research, 38*(4), 357–387.

McKee, P., Harrison, M. L., McCowen, A., Lehr, E., & Durr, W. (1966). *Reading for meaning* (4th ed.). Boston: Houghton Mifflin.

National Institute of Child Health and Human Development. (2000). *Report of the National Reading Panel: Teaching children to read: An evidence-based assessment of the scientific research literature on reading and its implications for reading instruction: Reports of the subgroups.* Washington, DC: Author.

Pinnell, G. S., Pikulski, J. J., Wixson, K. K., Campbell, J. R., Gough, P. B., & Beatty, A. S. (1995). *Listening to children read aloud: Data from NAEP's integrated reading performance record (IRPR) at grade 4.* Washington, DC: Office of Educational Research and Improvement, Department of Education. Princeton, NJ: Educational Testing Service.

Rashotte, C., & Torgesen, J. K. (1985). Repeated reading and reading fluency in learning disabled children. *Reading Research Quarterly, 20,* 180–188.

Rathman, P. (1995). *Officer Buckle and Gloria.* New York: Putnam Juvenile.

Rayner, K. (1977). Visual attention in reading: Eye movements reflect cognitive processes. *Memory and Cognition, 4,* 443–448.

Reutzel, R. (2005, May 1). *Developing fluency in classroom settings.* Paper presented at the annual meeting of the International Reading Association, San Antonio, TX.

Rowland, P. T. (1982). *The nitty gritty city.* Menlo Park, CA: Addison-Wesley.

Samuels, S. J. (1979). The method of repeated readings. *The Reading Teacher, 32,* 403–408.

Snow, C. E., Griffin, P., & Burns, M. S. (Eds.). (2005). *Knowledge to support the teaching of reading.* San Francisco: Jossey-Bass.

Stahl, S. A., & Heubach, K. M. (2005). Fluency-oriented reading. *Journal of Literacy Research, 37,* 25–60.

Stefoff, R. (1998). *Ants.* New York: Benchmark Books.

Thompson, G. B., Cottrell, D. S., & Fletcher-Flinn, C. M. (1996). Sublexical orthographic–phonological relations early in the acquisition of reading: The knowledge sources account. *Journal of Experimental Child Psychology, 62,* 190–222.

Wiederholt, J. L., & Bryant, B. R. (2001). *Gray Oral Reading Test* (4th ed.). Austin, TX: PRO-ED.

Wylie, R. E., & Durrell, D. D. (1970). Teaching vowels through phonograms. *Elementary English, 47,* 787–791.

Zeno, S. M., Ivens, S. H., Millard, R. T., & Duvvuri, R. (1995). *The educator's word frequency guide.* New York: Touchstone Applied Science.

Glossary

Adult fictive kin—adults who, although not related by blood or marriage, live with a child.

Affix—a word unit that is attached to the beginning (prefix) or the end (suffix) of a root or base word to modify its meaning (e.g., the "s" in *cats* or the "un" in *unclear*).

Age/grade equivalent—scores that are computed based on the average performance of every age group, or grade-reference group, used in the normative sample.

Alternate-forms reliability—an index that compares two equivalent forms of the same instrument to ensure that each is measuring the same attribute in a similar way.

Antiphonal choral reading—the choral or unison reading of sections of a text by two or more groups of readers.

Attainment value—an individual's perceived importance of attaining a particular goal (this is often influenced by the degree to which those around the person—teachers, family, and friends—value that goal).

Authentic themed unit—a unit of instruction based upon a major idea or proposition that arises from the topics covered in content areas along with literature or language arts texts.

Automaticity—the ability to perform any skilled behavior easily, with little attention, effort, or conscious awareness. Skills become automatic after extended periods of practice.

Automatize—to convert a slow, often inaccurate, resource-demanding task into one that can be completed quickly, easily, and with little conscious effort or attention.

Blend—to combine individual sounds to make a word.

Blending—the ability to put the phonemes identified through the use of phonics together to form words.

Challenge words—multisyllabic words that consist of taught orthographic patterns such as rimes, affixes, consonant blends and digraphs, and common vowel clusters. These words are presented to students to provide practice in applying decoding strategies.

Choice—the selection of one activity, thing, or person rather than another.

Choral reading—the practice in which both the teacher and the students read the text aloud in unison.

Connected text—longer written texts that communicate meaning, such as that found in books, poems, compositions, newspapers, etc.; usually contrasted with single-word, single-sentence, or random word lists.

Construct validity—the degree to which a test measures the construct, trait, or variable of interest.

Content validity—the extent to which a test appropriately samples a given domain.

Conversation groups—student-generated conversations about specific themes or issues in a text.

Core deficits—deficits in the speech and language domain that lead to the inability of some learners to process either the sounds in words or to rapidly retrieve the name of a given item, and usually result in difficulties in learning to read.

Criterion (predictive) validity—indicates the degree to which a score on a test predicts an individual's score or performance in some other area.

Criterion-referenced assessment—tests interpretation with reference to a specified content domain.

Decoding—the analysis of written words by determining their sound–symbol correspondences.

Double deficit—learners who have both phonological and naming speed deficits.

Dyslexia—a developmental reading disability that is likely to be congenital or present from birth.

Echo reading—the practice in which the teacher reads a section of the text (several sentences or a paragraph) aloud, and the students read it back in unison.

Effort—how hard a person is willing to work at an activity.

Elaborated vocabulary lesson—vocabulary instruction that includes definitional, contextual, and relational information, active student participation, and multiple exposures to terms.

Explicit instruction—instruction that is direct and clearly specified.

Families—children and their adult caretakers who provide care for the children in the children's residence. A family may include parents (most often), older siblings, grandparents, stepparents, foster parents, or other adult fictive kin.

Family literacy programs—programs designed to break the cycle of low literacy by offering parents instruction in their children's literacy development. Typically, these programs provide information on strategies that support literacy development, and sometimes help parents build their own literacy skills.

Fluency—*see* Reading fluency.

Fluent reading—*see* Reading fluency.

Garden variety poor readers—children who perform poorly at most of the subskills engaged in by reading.

Goals for reading—what an individual wants to achieve in his or her reading.

Gradient texts—a ranking based upon progressive change in texts' difficulty level (e.g., grade levels, guided reading levels).

Gradual release of responsibility—the lessening of support on the part of the teacher over the course of time in order to allow a learner to take on increasing responsibility for a task.

Guided reading—the use of instructional-level texts in a small-group format to assist students in the development of specific strategies (e.g., word recognition, comprehension, vocabulary development).

Heavy texts—texts that are complex in terms of concepts and vocabulary and are relatively lengthy (e.g., a complex picture book as opposed to a less conceptually challenging and more easily decodable text).

Home–school programs—a term broader than just family literacy programs these programs are designed to promote positive connections between the students' families and their school through a range of social and academic foci.

Informational text—a nonfiction book that presents a set of facts related to a particular subject.

Inquiry projects—a student project, based on independent reading and research, designed to develop a learner's understanding of a particular subject.

Interest value—the extent to which a child is interested in carrying out a particular activity.

Intrinsic motivation—motivation that occurs because of some internal drive that the child has, often either because it is pleasurable, important, or otherwise significant.

Macrolevel comprehension—an understanding of the larger ideas and themes of a text.

Mastery goal—goal for learning that focuses on improvement of ability or skill.

Matthew effects—the notion that, because good readers engage in reading with much greater frequency than do struggling readers, the achievement gap between them becomes larger over time.

Metacognitive—the awareness of one's own mental processes that allows one to monitor learning (e.g., being able to go back and reread something when one has lost track of its meaning).

Microlevel comprehension—an understanding of a particular section (or ideas in a section) of a text.

Mnemonic—a device or strategy designed to improve a person's memory.

Modeling—a skilled person serving as an example for a learner.

Motivation—the force within a person that drives or directs behavior.

Naming speed deficit—the inability of a learner to rapidly access and retrieve names for visual symbols.

Narrative text—a story, whether factually based (e.g., a biography) or fiction.

Norm-referenced assessment—scores are compared to some standard or norm.

Normal distribution—a theoretical frequency distribution of measurements whereby scores are concentrated near the center (or mean) and decrease in frequency as the distance from the mean increases.

Orthographic patterns—the standard spelling patterns that are present in a writing system.

Paired reading—pairing of a more capable reader with a less capable one for the purposes of reading text aloud.

Partner reading—the pairing of children for the purpose of reading a text, with each student taking turns as both the reader and a helper.

Percentile rank—an indication of the relative position of a particular score within the norm group.

Performance goal—goal for learning that focuses on demonstrating superior performance in contrast to others.

Persistence—how long someone is willing to exert effort in an activity when he or she is having difficulty.

Phoneme deletion—the ability to remove a phoneme from a word.

Phoneme segmentation—the ability to identify individual phonemes in a word.

Phoneme substitution—the ability to exchange one phoneme for another.

Phonemes—the smallest sound units composing spoken language that can be combined to form words, for example, the words *cat* and *ship* both have three phonemes (/c/ /a/ /t/), (/sh/ /i/ /p/), whereas *trip* has four (/t/ /r/ /i/ /p/).

Phonemic awareness—an awareness of the individual sounds that make up a word.

Phonics—the relationship between phonemes (the sounds in *spoken* language) and letters or multiletter units that can be used to read or decode words.

Phonogram (or rime)—the part of the syllable that consists of the vowel and the letters that follow it (e.g., the -*at* in *sat*; the -*eat* in *treat*).

Phonological awareness—metacognitive knowledge about and sensitivity to the sound system of language.

Phonological deficits—an inability to identify the sounds that comprise words (e.g., syllables, onsets and rimes, and phonemes).

Phonological memory code—codes in memory that hold information about sounds and their typical patterns.

Power law of practice—mathematical function that describes the fact that people initially make large gains in skill as they practice, but that eventually these gains become smaller with subsequent practice.

Prosodic reading—expressive reading that makes use of pitch, emphasis, tempo, and appropriate phrasing.

Prosody—tonal and rhythmic aspects of reading, such as pitch, emphasis, loudness, and pauses, often used synonymously with expression.

Rate-limited comprehension—reading quickly, but not so quickly that the speed interferes with comprehension.

Raw score—total number of points earned on a test.

Reading fluency—combines quick and accurate word recognition with basic comprehension and expression that reflects the grammar of the sentence.

Reading rate—the speed with which an individual reads a text.

Reading with expression or prosody—involves the tonal and rhythmic aspects of reading, such as pitch, stress, loudness, and pauses.

Rime—*See* Phonogram.

Round robin reading (also, popcorn, popsicle, and combat reading)—the practice of asking individual students to read aloud short sections of a text (a sentence or a paragraph), one student following another.

Scaffolded repeated reading—the use of the support or assistance of a model (a teacher, more skilled reader, tape, or even CD ROM) to help a student read a challenging text repeatedly.

Scaffolded texts—texts and books designed to support the development of reading because of their unique features, such as texts focusing on a specific phonics pattern or containing mainly high-frequency words, etc.

Scaffolding—the provision of instructional supports in order to help learners acquire skills, complete tasks, or achieve a goal that is beyond their ability to complete independently.

Scaled score—a common type of standard score that has been popularized for use with specific subtests or domains. Scaled scores have a mean of 10 and a standard deviation of 3.

Self-efficacy—an individual's assessment of his or her own ability to succeed in accomplishing a given activity.

Semantic knowledge—knowledge of the meaning of words, phrases, and larger units of language.

Shared reading—the strategy of using a single text with a group of children to ensure that they all develop a common base of knowledge or understanding, be it about a specific strategy or a particular topic (e.g., developing directionality, working on a common comprehension strategy, developing knowledge about a historic event).

Sight vocabulary—all the words within a reader's lexicon.

Sight words—words that a child can read instantly rather than through the conscious use of phonics.

Standard deviation—a measure of the average distance of the test scores from the mean.

Standard score—a raw score converted to a normal distribution with a set mean and a standard deviation that has equal units along the scale. Standard scores have a mean of 100 and a standard deviation of 15.

Standardized assessments—assessments that adhere to clearly specified administration and scoring procedures.

Struggling readers—students who experience difficulties with some aspect of their reading development.

Test–retest reliability—an index that reflects the consistency of test results on two separate administrations.

Text reading fluency—the ability to read *connected text* with quick and accurate word recognition, basic comprehension, and expression.

Text structure—the patterns that exist in the organization of a text (e.g., cause-effect, problem–solution).

Treatment resisters—students who have particularly intransigent difficulties when learning to read and seem unable to benefit from interventions that help most children.

Unison reading—another term for choral reading.

Utility value—the perceived usefulness of a particular activity for the child.

Value for reading—an amalgamation of an individual's interest, attainment, and utility value for reading.

Vowel chunk—the vowel and the letters that come after it.

Webbing—the use of diagrams to show the relationship between various concepts.

Word callers—children who are able to recognize words readily but are unable to simultaneously comprehend what they are "reading."

Word reading autonomy—effortless reading of words that is unintended but difficult to avoid because of extensive practice.

Word reading efficiency—quick and accurate word reading skills.

Word zone—a classification of word frequency ranges in terms of words per million in running texts across a variety of text genre, designed to distinguish words in terms of their general frequency in written English.

Index

"f" following a page number indicates a figure;
"t" following a page number indicates a table.